Together *through* the Bible

Resources for All-age Worship

Together *through* the Bible

Resources for All-age Worship

Edited by Pam Macnaughton and Hamish Bruce

Illustrations by Simon Smith

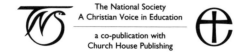

The National Society
A Christian Voice in Education

a co-publication with
Church House Publishing

Church House Publishing
Church House
Great Smith Street
London SW1P 3NZ

ISBN 0 7151 4907 5

Published in 1998 by The National Society and Church House Publishing

Compilation copyright © *The National Society (Church of England) for Promoting Religious Education* 1998.

Individual items contained in this book are copyright © Catherine A. Olodude, Christopher Smith, Christopher Herbert, Betty Pedley, Jenny Willis, Claire Roberts, Leslie Noon, Robert Cuin, Sheila Jacobs, Jane Whitcroft, Margaret Gregory, Barbara Hastings Cox, Sheila Forsdyke, Peter Comaish, Jean Ball, Dorothy Morris, Malcolm Williams, John and Ruth Tiller, Paul Thomas, Donald Dowling, Jon Webster, Barbara Rohde, Adrian Legg, James Bryce, Anthony Geering, Judith Sadler, Dave Hopwood, Don Tordoff, Simon Marshall, Susan Skinner, Derek Haylock, Joy Blaylock, Sue and Hamish Bruce, Pauline Lewis.

Illustrations copyright © *Simon Smith*

Acknowledgements

Extracts from *An Alternative Order for Public Baptism of Infants* (1990) and *An Alternative Order for Morning and Evening Prayer* (1992) are copyright © The Church in Wales 1990, 1992 and are reproduced by permission.

Cover design by Julian Smith

Printed in England by Biddles Ltd, Guildford and King's Lynn

Contents

The Old Testament

Creation   3

Noah   13

Joseph   23

Exodus/Moses   32

Teachings of Jesus 83

Events of Jesus' life 106

Passion / Easter 119

Pentecost 136

Acts   **147**

Revelation   **158**

Introduction

If you are planning a worship service, or an assembly or special occasion with children, or with all ages on a specific theme or character from the Bible, often just what you need is something to bring it to life. This book is for you. Well-loved Bible characters take their place here: praying, laughing, praising, running away, obeying, being afraid, and demonstrating remarkable faith. All of them have something to teach us about God's relationship and dealing with people.

So in a variety of resources you will find ideas to spark off new approaches to the stories in the Bible that nurture our faith. If you are a subscriber to *Together with Children* magazine, you may well recognize some of this material, but a third has been especially commissioned for this book. (Further details about the magazine can be found at the back of the book.) We hope that the material will help you to explore the Bible with children in new and imaginative ways.

Pam Macnaughton

Editor, *Together with Children*

Hamish Bruce

Anthology Editor

List of Abbreviations

BBC CP	*BBC Come and Praise*, BBC Books, 1978
CFC	*Carols for Choirs 3*, Oxford University Press, 1978
CHFE	*Celebration Hymnal for Everyone*, McCrimmons, 1994
CFW	Michael Perry (ed.), *Church Family Worship*, Hodder and Stoughton, 1986
HAMNS	*Hymns Ancient and Modern New Standard*, Hymns Ancient and Modern Limited, 1983
HON	*Hymns Old and New*, New Anglican Edition, Kevin Mayhew, 1996
HTC	*Hymns for Today's Church,* Hodder and Stoughton, 1982
JP	*Junior Praise,* Combined Music Edition, Marshall Pickering, 1997
MP	*Mission Praise*, Marshall Pickering, 1986
OBC	*The Oxford Book of Carols*, Oxford University Press, 1964
SHF	*Songs and Hymns of Fellowship,* Integrated Music Edition, Kingsway Music, 1987
SNOBC	*The Shorter New Oxford Book of Carols*, Oxford University Press, 1993

Acknowledgements

The publisher gratefully acknowledges permission to reproduce copyright material in this book. Every effort has been made to trace and contact copyright holders. If there are any inadvertent omissions we apologize to those concerned and will ensure that a suitable acknowledgement is made at the next reprint.

Prayers by Christopher Herbert from *Prayers for Children* (National Society/Church House Publishing, 1993) are copyright © Christopher Herbert 1993 and are reproduced by permission (p.9).

The Bible quotations are taken from the *Good News Bible* published by the Bible Societies and HarperCollins Publishers, © American Bible Society 1994. Used by permission. All rights reserved.

THE OLD TESTAMENT

Creation

Evening and morning

This short creation sketch works best with at least twelve children, or fewer children and adults for the speaking parts. Make sure the children are well rehearsed to keep the sketch moving. As each child enters with their visual aid, they bow to the Voice of God. You might want to use background music for this sketch.

Bible reference

Genesis 1 – 2

Cast

Voice of God, Chorus, Man, Bearers of visual aids

Props

The props needed are large cards with pictures of the main categories of the creation story, except vegetation which can be represented by bowls of fruit, pots of flowers, and plants

Voice   Let there be light!

(Enter child carrying card showing Light. The child bows before the Voice of God.)

Chorus   And there was evening and there was morning, the first day.

(Exit Light.)

Voice   Sky! Come from among the waters.

(Enter child carrying card showing Sky.)

Chorus   And there was evening and there was morning, the second day.

(*Exit Sky.*)

Voice   Waters! Come together and be called seas.

(*Enter child carrying card showing Sea.*)

Dry land! Come out and be called Earth. Bring out all sorts of trees, plants and fruits.

(*Enter child representing Earth, with the fruit, flowers and plants.*)

Chorus   And there was evening, and there was morning, the third day.

(*Exit Earth and Sea.*)

Voice   Lights! Separate the day from the night and be signs for spring, summer, autumn and winter for a very long time.

(*Enter Light again, with two cards: day and night. The 'day' one can include illustrations for the different seasons.*)

Chorus   And there was evening, and there was morning, the fourth day.

(*Exit Light.*)

Voice   Waters! I want you to bring forth lots of sea animals.

(*Enter Sea again with another card filled with pictures of sea animals.*)

Birds! From this day, start flying above the earth across the heavens.

4

(*Enter child with card showing bird in flight.*)

Water, animals and birds, I bless you. Begin to multiply.

Chorus And there was evening, and there was morning, the fifth day.

(*Exit Sea and Bird.*)

Voice Earth! Now bring out cattle, dogs, lions, hens, cats, gorillas, tigers, cheetahs, reindeer, rabbits, elephants, butterflies, cockroaches, ants, spiders, and everything I have dreamed.

(*Enter Earth again with colourful illustrations of these animals.*)

Now, it is time to make man.

(*Enter a boy. He too bows.*)

Man, I give you power over every other thing I have made. Be blessed. Multiply, eat of every green plant and their fruit.

(*Lays his hand on the child's head in an act of blessing.*)

Man Thank you, dear Lord.

Chorus And there was morning, and there was evening, the sixth day.

(*Exit boy.*)

Voice I am glad to finish making everything in heaven and earth. They are very, very good. Now I can have some rest.

Seventh day!

(*Enter a child with 'seventh day' pinned on his T-shirt. The Voice of God holds his hands.*)

I bless you. I make you a day of rest and holier than the other days that I used for my work.

(*Exit child.*)

(*All the children come back together, holding their cards, props or hands high.*)

All   God has now completed his work. Everything he has made is good indeed.

(*It works well to finish off the sketch by singing* 'All things bright and beautiful', HTC 283.)

Catherine A. Olodude

The creation rap

This rap might be performed by a small group of children, to a simple drum beat. Use the words in italics as a repetitive refrain as a break between each of the 'verses'.

Bible reference

Genesis 1 – 2

Searching the Bible can be lots of fun,
When we read it we find what God has done.
Let's open it first at Genesis ONE,
Then we'll know our search has really begun.

Praise God, praise, praise, praise, etc.

God made the sun and he made the stars,
He made the planets, Jupiter and Mars.
He set them in heaven, shining so bright,
The sun in the day and the moon at night.

Praise God, praise, praise, praise, etc.

He created the birds, the trees and plants,
He made hippopotami and tiny ants.
Insects and animals, great and small,
We thank him for creating them all.

Thank God, thank, thank, thank, etc.

For creating the cows that give us milk,
And for silkworms producing their silk.
Honey bees, snails, giraffes so tall,
We thank him for creating them all.

Thank God, thank, thank, thank, etc.

For big oak trees and mountain spruce,
For the duck, the moorhen and the goose.
For butterflies bright with colourful wings,
For the skylark's song and the joy that it brings.

Thank God, thank, thank, thank, etc.

Dear Father in heaven, we thank you each one,
For the wonderful things that you have done,
But the most wonderful thing must surely be,
You created my parents and you created ME!

Christopher Smith

Creation prayers

1.   Father, you have made the world very beautiful.

Teach us to love our world,

and to treat it with reverence and with care,

for Jesus' sake.

Amen.

2.   Let there be light:

the light of the moon,

the light of the sun,

light on the waters,

light in the clouds,

light in the mountains,

light on the leaves of the shimmering trees.

Let there be light . . .

And it was good.

'*Yes*,' dear God, to the light.

Amen.

Christopher Herbert

Two craft activities

These two simple craft activities would be ideal for children's activity groups. 'Say it with flowers' would also be appropriate for Mothering Sunday.

1.   The gifts of God – a creation tree

You will need:

Hole-punch

Crayons or felt-tips

Small lengths of fine thread

Photocopied templates

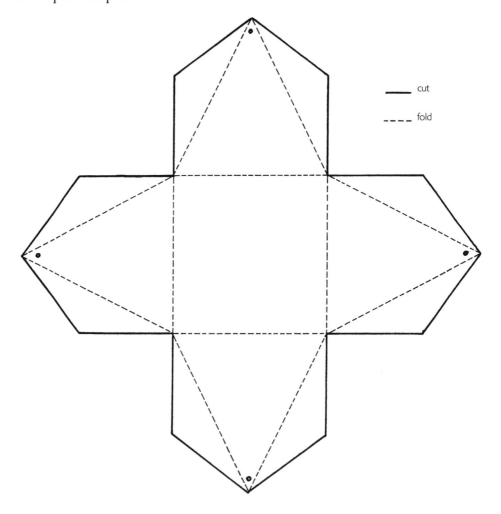

cut

fold

(a) Enlarge the given template on a photocopier. Then use it to cut out shapes using brightly coloured card. Fold the shape along all the lines. Older children could do this for themselves but it is helpful if the leader prepares the cardboard shapes to this stage for use by younger children.

(b) Punch a small hole in each of the triangles where a circle is drawn.

On the outward faces of the shape (one square, four triangles), the children draw their own pictures of the different parts of creation, (darkness/light, sea, land, sun, moon, stars, etc.). Ensure that the children draw themselves on one of the faces.

(c) Fold the shape with all the flaps turned inwards and the pictures on the outside. Run a length of thread or fine string through the holes and tie it to secure the shapes as a pyramid.

(d) Hang all the children's pyramids from a branch and make a tree laden with the gifts of creation.

2. Say it with flowers

You will need:
Brightly coloured thin card or poster paper
Scissors
Felt-tips or crayons
Masking tape or cloth tape
Garden canes
Small plant pots filled with soil

(a) Using brightly coloured poster paper or thin card, cut out large petals and a circle for the middle of each flower. The petals can be different shapes and numbers per flower.

(b) Children draw pictures of beautiful things in God's creation on the petals and a picture of themselves on the circle in the centre.

Assemble the petals to make a flower.

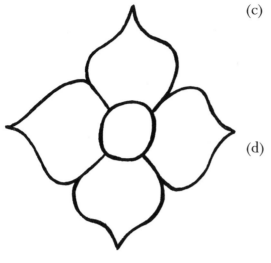

(c) Tape the back of the flower to a short, thin garden cane using masking tape or cloth tape. Leaves can be attached to the garden cane. Stick the base of the cane into a small plant pot (10–15 cm deep) filled with soil.

(d) Around the pot stick a strip of paper bearing the prayer

'Thank you God for your wonderful world.

Please help me to look after it.'

Betty Pedley

Noah

Noah crafts

These craft activities to celebrate the story of Noah will give children great enjoyment and result in some impressive end products. They will need to be done over more than one session, to allow time for baking or the drying of varnish.

Bible reference

Genesis 6 – 8

For the five- to seven-year-olds

Mr Noah wellie peg

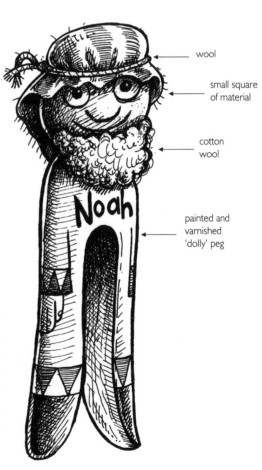

wool

small square of material

cotton wool

painted and varnished 'dolly' peg

You will need:

An old-fashioned wooden peg, sometimes called a 'dolly' peg

A small square of material, about 8 cm square (striped looks best)

A piece of wool

A ball of cotton wool

Glue

Poster paints

Varnish

Very carefully paint Noah's eyes. Paint in his coat and hands using strong bright colours. A pattern around the bottom of his coat and sleeves is very effective. Paint or write with felt-pen his name on the front. When the paint is dry, varnish the pegs – this is definitely a job for the adults! When the varnish is dry, stick on a cotton-wool beard with glue. Dab a little glue on the top of Noah's head, and, using the piece of wool, tie the square of material onto his head. This is rather fiddly and children will need help.

The children can take the pegs home to keep their wellies together. Every time it rains, they can remember the story of Noah.

For the seven- to nine-year-olds

Noah mobile

You will need:
Thin card
Thread or fine string
Scissors
Paints, felt-tips or crayons

The shapes for the mobile can be drawn freehand by the children, choosing their own animals. It is a good idea to draw round a large plate to get a good curve for the rainbow. It is also important to make sure that the ark is small enough to fit inside the curve of the rainbow. Alternatively, the design opposite can be enlarged on a photocopier and templates made. Cut out the pictures and colour in or paint them on both sides with plenty of bold colours.

Make holes carefully at the top and bottom of each shape. (Noah and the pigs need a hole only at the top.) Try to make sure the holes line up under each other. Varnish the pictures for added effect and durability if wanted. Copying the diagram here, join all the shapes together with strong thread or fine string. Do it with the pieces all laid out flat on a table, to avoid getting in a muddle.

The mobile can be hung up in a bedroom or would make an excellent gift for a baby or younger child.

cut alternate slots

cut alternate slots

For the eight-year-olds and over

Salt dough pendants

You will need:
Plain white flour
Salt
Cooking oil
Water
Mixing bowl and wooden spoon
Rolling pin
Poster paints and brush
Varnish
Knife

Mix equal amounts of salt and flour in the bowl. Add a little cooking oil and enough water to make a dough. Knead until the dough is soft and stretchy. Roll out the dough, not too thin, until it is flat and smooth.

For the rainbow pendants

Use a pastry cutter, or a lid or mug, to cut out the round shape, about 8 cm across. If necessary, neaten the shape with a knife. Use a knitting needle or pencil to make a hole near the top.

Leave it to dry a little for 24 hours, then bake in a very slow oven for several hours until it is very hard. Take care not to burn it.

For the dove

Very carefully copy the design, or photocopy the design and make a template. Making little holes with a cocktail stick is a good way to draw on dough. Then cut out the shape with a knife.

As with the other design, make a hole, dry it and bake it. When the dough shapes are cold, paint them with poster paints, then finish with a coat of varnish. Thread a ribbon or leather strip through the hole.

Jenny Willis

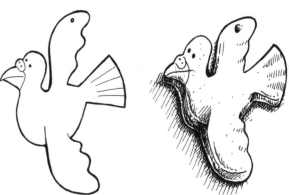

Man or maniac?

Noah leaves the audience guessing in this sketch. It requires only two actors and follows the format of a TV chat show. It could easily lead to discussion with older children and adults about hearing and obeying the promptings of God. This sketch is relatively quick to put together and only involves minimal props.

Bible reference

Genesis 6.5 – 7.16

Cast

Interviewer and Noah, some primed members of the audience

Props

Raincoat, wellies, large umbrella

Interviewer Good evening, and welcome to *Man or Maniac?* Tonight's guest, ladies and gentlemen, is a man whose astonishing and unusual action is currently taking the world by storm. While peoples of every nation are panic-buying suntan lotions, he is in the process of building the world's largest boat . . . to live on. So all the way from the middle of the desert, let's give a big warm welcome to Noah.

(Noah enters wearing a raincoat, wellies and carrying a large umbrella. The interviewer, along with the audience, claps Noah to his seat. Noah holds out his hands to acknowledge the applause.)

Interviewer First of all, Mr Noah . . .

Noah No *Mister*. Just Noah. *(Beams at interviewer.)*

Interviewer Fine . . .

Noah *(Holding out his hand and looking up)* Not for much longer.

Interviewer *(Laughs uncertainly)* Before we start, Noah, I would like to thank you on behalf of everyone here for taking time out from your boat . . .

Noah Ark!

Interviewer Bless you.

Noah It's not a boat, it's an ark.

Interviewer *(Slight pause)* Oh. . . an ark.

Noah Yes, that's right.

Interviewer Yes. . .um. . .on your *ark* building project *(Noah gives interviewer the thumbs up)* to come to chat to us this evening.

Noah My pleasure. *(Beams around at everyone)* What exactly would you like to chat about?

Interviewer Basically, why you're building this big, huge bo . . . er . . . ark.

Noah What do you mean 'why'?

Interviewer Well, why in the middle of the driest desert, during the longest drought ever, are you building this ark?

Noah Because it's going to rain.

(Hysterical laughter from interviewer and audience.)

Interviewer Forgive us, Noah, for laughing. It's just that even if it were going to rain, which is highly unlikely in itself, how much rain are you expecting?

Noah	A worldful.
Interviewer	A worldful?
Noah	Yes, it's going to rain non stop for forty days and forty nights . . .
Interviewer	Forty days and forty nights?
Noah	Yes, and the whole world will be flooded.
Interviewer	And why exactly do you think it will rain for this length of time?
Noah	I don't think . . . I know.
Interviewer	(*Slightly irritable*) And how do you know?
Noah	God told me.
Interviewer	(*Mouth open, glances at the audience*) *God* told you?
Noah	Yes. I was out one morning whe . . .
Interviewer	Were you wearing a sun hat?
Noah	(*Pause*) No. I was out walking one . . .
Interviewer	Do you ever wear a sun hat? (*Audience laughter.*)
Noah	(*Cross*) Why are you interested in my head gear? Here I am telling you . . .or trying to tell you that God spoke to me with a warning of imminent danger, and all you're concerned about is what I had on my head at the time. I don't know! The people of this day and age are unbelievable. No wonder God wants to get rid of you all and save the animals.
Interviewer	Did God tell you that as well?
Noah	Yes, we had a good talk actually.
Interviewer	Let me get this straight. You were out walking one hot sunny morning, without your sun hat (*Noah rolls his eyes*) and God tells you it's going to rain and you must build an ark to save the animals from drowning, but not the people.
Noah	(*Sarcastically*) Oh, so you have been listening to some of what I've been saying then.
Interviewer	And how many animals do you propose taking on board?
Noah	Two of every kind.
Interviewer	*Every* kind?
Noah	Yes, because we wouldn't want any to become extinct.

Interviewer (*Playing-along type voice*) Of course we wouldn't. And where are these herds of animals all going to go? It must be a very big ark.

Noah (*Enthusiastically*) It is. It's 133 metres long, 22 metres wide, and 13 metres high . . . with a roof. Spared no expense.

Interviewer (*Same tone*) And I suppose God gave you the measurements as well, did he?

Noah Yes . . . who else . . .

Interviewer (*Same tone*) Of course he did.

Noah (*Beaming again*) Oh, I'm so pleased. I was beginning to think that you didn't believe me. That you thought I was mad . . . hearing voices. You wouldn't believe the reaction I'm getting from people. I told them, 'Listen to God.' I told them, 'You must build arks for yourselves too.' 'Listen to God,' I told them, 'or you'll drown.'

Interviewer Quite right, Noah. And what did they say?

Noah They laughed.

Interviewer Unbelievable. Well, thank you once again, Noah, for sparing us your valuable time this evening. Goodbye, oh and good luck with all those animals.

Noah Thank you! Goodbye. Goodbye everyone.

(*Noah leaves amid applause and laughter.*)

Interviewer There you have it, ladies and gentlemen, and we finish tonight with those immortal words still ringing in our ears, 'Listen to God, or you will drown.' Make up your own minds, ladies and gentlemen . . . *Man or Maniac?*

Claire Roberts

The rainbow rap

This version of Noah's story is a great chance for junior-aged children to show off their rapping skills. Get the smaller children to learn the chorus so everyone can join in.

Bible reference

Genesis 6 – 9

Chorus   *Come on everybody, we've a story to tell*
'Bout a great big flood and a rainbow as well.
There's Noah and his wife and children too,
And on board ship there's even a zoo.

We read in the Bible that once upon a time,
The people on earth were very unkind.
They fought, they lied, they were generally bad,
God saw this and it made him sad.

Chorus

The people were selfishly destroying God's world,
So God spoke to Noah, his plan he unfurled.
Build a big boat with lots of room,
And be prepared, it will rain very soon.

Chorus

Noah did what God had told him,
People laughed as they watched him building.
The birds and the beasts were quickly installed,
Then came the rains as God foretold.

Chorus

The puddles grew bigger, they began to float,
Safe from the flood on Noah's big boat.
There they stayed till the waters went down,
And the ark came to rest on solid ground.

Chorus

There in the sky was a wonderful scene,
A glorious rainbow which we know to mean
A promise from God – that for evermore
He will guard the world – and that's for sure.

Leslie Noon

Joseph

Horrible little brother

A sketch introducing people to the first part of the epic life-story of Joseph.

Bible reference
Genesis 37

Cast
Joseph, Brother 1, Brother 2

Joseph   Hi there, brothers. Do you want to hear about the dream I had last night?

Brother 1	No!
Joseph	Well, I'll tell you anyway. I'm sure you'll be interested. I dreamt that we were all working in the fields.
Brother 2	I once dreamt that you were working. But as you know, that sort of dream never comes true.
Brother 1	Yes, how can anyone work in such a ridiculous coat?
Brother 2	Talk about Daddy's little favourite . . .
Joseph	Anyway, in my dream I made a sheaf of corn, and all your sheaves bowed down to it.
Brother 1	Stupid dream if you ask me. About as stupid as the guy who dreamt it.
Brother 2	Hang on – you don't mean to say that you're imagining that we will all worship you one day? Fat chance of that!
	(*Joseph wanders off muttering to himself.*)
Brother 1	I hate that lad. Even more so because he is obviously Dad's favourite. One of these days when Father's not looking . . .
Brother 2	Yeah. We ought to rough him up a bit, show him what we think about him and his dreams. Do some damage to that silly coat as well.
	(*Some days later.*)
Joseph	I had another dream last night. Do you want me to tell it to you?
Brother 1	No! But I suppose as usual you will anyway.
Joseph	I dreamt that the sun, the moon and the stars all bowed down to me.
Brother 1	What sort of stupid dream is that? Do you think that even your father as well as all of us will one day worship you? You've got to be joking!
Brother 2	(*Whispers*) How about we get him now? Do something just to bring him down a peg?
Brother 1	(*Whispers*) Just wait, our time will come. Then we can be rid of this upstart once and for all.
	(*Some time later. The brothers are out in the country looking after the sheep. Joseph comes along to see them.*)
Joseph	(*Calls out from distance*) Hello, hello there!

Brother 1   That looks like Joseph coming this way.

Brother 2   Oh no, not more of his dreams I hope.

Brother 1   Hey, Father's not around, now's our chance to get the little horror.

Brother 2   You don't mean to kill him, do you? Can't we just rough him up a bit and show that we don't like his tales?

Brother 1   Yes, just rough him up a bit. Then he runs back to his dad and squeals to him about what we've done. You know all this began with him telling tales on us. Do you want to give him ammunition to use against us? No, we should be rid of him once and for all.

Brother 2   We could drop him into this pit, throw in a few scorpions and snakes, and then say a wild animal must have eaten him.

Brother 1   No, wait. I've a better idea. See that camel train over there?

Brother 2   Yes, the one that passes here every month you mean?

Brother 1   Yes, that's the one. You know what the owner of those camels does, don't you?

Brother 2   Buys and sells slaves.

Brother 1   Exactly. We could sell our dear little brother to that slave trader. We get some cash. We get rid of Joseph. We have a party with the money. We tell his dad that he was eaten by wolves or something.

Brother 2   And we say how sorry we are.

Brother 1   Meanwhile some poor Egyptian has to put up with Joseph and his dreams.

Brother 2   Yes, an excellent idea. He won't last long in Egypt. Not if he starts telling them about his stupid dreams.

Robert Cuin

25

God's good plan

Bible reference

Genesis 40 – 41

The story of Joseph's imprisonment and eventual release and rise to fame is told from an unusual source – Pharaoh's chief cupbearer.

There's nothing worse than famine. The terrible hunger, desperate people doing desperate things. It could have been like that here, in Egypt.

I'm the chief cupbearer to Pharaoh, king of Egypt. I can't remember what I did to annoy him, all those years ago, but I was slung into jail, along with the chief baker, and the captain of the guard said a man called Joseph would be in charge of us while we were in prison.

'Joseph!' I whispered to the baker. 'I've heard of him. Isn't he a Hebrew slave? Didn't Potiphar the official put him in charge of his whole household? Why is Joseph in prison?'

'Why? Because I was falsely charged,' said a voice from behind us, 'and falsely imprisoned.'

I turned round and saw a well-built, handsome young man. His stern face broke into a smile.

That was the beginning of my friendship with Joseph. I learned quite a lot about him. He had been sold into slavery by his own brothers. I often wondered why he wasn't bitter and angry, but he just said that God had a purpose in everything that happened to him and that it would all work out for good in the end.

Then, one night, I had a strange dream.

'What a terrible night!' I said to the chief baker the next morning. 'I had a dream, and I'm sure it had some meaning. I've never had a dream like it before.'

'You had a dream, too, did you?' said the baker, looking miserable. 'So did I. It frightened the life out of me.'

'What a coincidence!' I said, and just then, Joseph came along, and asked us why we both looked so dejected.

'We've had dreams,' I sighed. 'We think they mean something, but who will interpret them for us?'

Then Joseph told us to tell him our dreams, for he said that the interpretation of dreams belonged to God. So I told him about my dream and – to my surprise – he told me what my dream meant. He said that within three days I would be restored to my position by Pharaoh.

'And when that happens,' he said, 'remember me and tell Pharaoh about me, because I have done nothing wrong and do not deserve to be in this prison.'

Then the chief baker, seeing that Joseph said my dream promised good things, told Joseph his own dream. But Joseph did not have good news for him. He informed the chief baker that within three days he would be put to death by Pharaoh.

And I think the chief baker wished he'd never asked.

Well, within three days, what Joseph had foretold came true. It was Pharaoh's birthday, and he gave a feast for all his officials, and on that occasion he restored me to my position as chief cupbearer. But he had the chief baker put to death.

I was sorry for the chief baker, of course, but thrilled to be free. And I'm sorry to say, I was so thrilled, I completely forgot about Joseph and didn't tell Pharaoh about him.

It was two long years before I remembered Joseph. Then, one day, I was going about my business when I saw Pharaoh, long-faced and miserable, and I asked him what was wrong.

'I've had two dreams,' he said, 'and I can't find anyone in all Egypt who can interpret them.' It was then that I recalled Joseph, and I felt very guilty.

'What's the matter?' asked Pharaoh, frowning.

So I told him how I had had a dream when I was in prison, and how Joseph interpreted it for me, and how he had also told the chief baker what would happen to him – and both interpretations came true.

'I should have remembered Joseph before, and told Pharaoh about him as he asked me to,' I said to myself as Pharaoh sent for Joseph. 'It's been two years, and I could have helped him. If Pharaoh hadn't had those dreams, I might never have remembered Joseph at all.'

It's a good thing I did remember him, because Joseph came to Pharaoh, and heard his dreams, and interpreted them. One dream was about seven fat, sleek cows who came out of the river and grazed among the reeds. Then seven lean, ugly cows came and ate the sleek cows. The second dream was about seven ears of corn, full and good, growing on a single stalk. Then another seven ears sprouted, and they were withered and thin, and they swallowed up the seven good ears of corn.

Joseph said that the dreams were one and the same, and that God had revealed to Pharaoh what he was about to do.

'There will be seven years of great abundance in Egypt, followed by seven years of famine,' he said. He also advised Pharaoh that he should find a wise man to be in charge of Egypt, and to collect up the grain and store it during the seven good years, so that in the years of famine the people would not starve.

So Pharaoh put Joseph in charge and Joseph stored up the grain as he had said, so that the people of Egypt had something to eat during the years of famine. Not only did the people of Egypt have food but those of all the other lands that suffered famine came to Egypt to buy grain, too. Some of those people were Joseph's own family, the very brothers who had sold him into slavery all those years before.

I heard about their arrival, and how Joseph greeted them with forgiveness and love. I also heard that he told them that although they had intended to harm him, God had worked everything out for good in the end.

I think I would like to know this God of Joseph's who is so powerful and who cares so much about his people.

Sheila Jacobs

The story of Joseph

This interactive craft picture helps children to remember the story in sequence and to develop the concept of how we relate differently to all kinds of people and situations at different stages in our lives.

Bible reference

Genesis 37 – 50

You will need:

A1 rigid card

Scissors

Crayons and felt-tips

Velcro stickers

Divide the story of Joseph into episodes and choose the picture/symbol which will represent each episode. For example:

1. Joseph's coat
2. Joseph's dream (sun, moon, corn, etc.)
3. Joseph sold as a slave (camel train)
4. Joseph in prison (prison bars)
5. Pharaoh's dreams (fat and thin cows)
6. Joseph's important position (Ruler King)
7. Sacks of grain (silver cup, etc.)
8. Famine.

Decide whether you are going to make one large picture produced by the group or if children are to make individual pictures. The size of the large rigid card needed for the pictures will be determined by your decision. Large signs used by chain stores and supermarkets are ideal for this purpose. An individual picture needs to be at least A1 size and obviously a group picture or frieze would be very much bigger. Draw the twelve brothers increasing in size and stick them onto the centre of the board in size order, leaving a space where Joseph belongs (next to the youngest). In Joseph's place draw a black solid shape representing the outline shape of Joseph. Onto this black shape attach two Velcro stickers. Stick the Joseph figure onto thin card and stick two Velcro stickers on the back of this card shape so that they marry up to the ones on the black shape. Joseph can be stuck in his position in the family line-up or removed to go on his travels around the picture as the story progresses.

Start in the top right-hand corner and make the picture of the first episode in the story. This can be made separately using collage materials and interesting textured papers, etc. and then stuck in position. The first picture would be of Joseph's coat.

Next to the coat draw a black silhouette of Joseph. This should also have the two Velcro stickers put in position so that Joseph can be removed from his place in the family and attached to the board next to his coat.

On subsequent occasions as the different episodes of the story are told, moving clockwise round the board make the pictures of the different episodes. If interesting fabrics, foil, etc. are used the picture has a very tactile as well as visual attraction. Each picture episode should contain the black outline of Joseph complete with two Velcro stickers.

The different incidents in the story can be linked by footsteps drawn on the board.

Jane Whitcroft

Exodus/Moses

A most sensible sister

A fresh and exciting look at the story of Moses in the bulrushes. Younger children will enjoy just listening to it, but older ones may like to act or mime the story afterwards. It is certainly a reminder to all ages that children are just as important as adults in playing their part in the purposes of God. Who knows what would have happened to Moses and the people of Israel without Miriam?

Bible reference

Genesis 2.1-10

'Why are you making that basket?' Miriam asked, as she sat at home with her mother.

'We need it to hide your baby brother in,' Mother said, picking up the last bulrushes to weave into her basket. She sighed. 'Now that he is three months old, every time he cries I'm afraid our masters, the Egyptians, will hear him.'

Miriam nodded. 'And then they'll take him away – and throw him into the river.' She shuddered. 'Mother, why do the Egyptians hate our baby boys?'

'Oh child! The king of Egypt hates all the Hebrew people because there are so many of us. That's why he keeps us as slaves and works us almost to death.' She stroked Miriam's dark hair, adding, 'But one day, you'll see, the Lord God will save us.'

Mother finished her basket, making it waterproof, and placed the baby inside. He waved his arms in the air and kicked up his legs, and even Mother's anxious face broke into a smile.

The next morning, while it was still cool, she and Miriam went to the river. Mother was carrying her bulrush basket with the baby asleep inside. They found a quiet place beside the riverbank and hid the basket among the reeds. It floated in the shallow water.

'He'll be safer here,' Mother said. 'Now listen, child,' she told Miriam, 'you play by the river, some way off from your brother. But watch out, to see if anyone comes this way.' Mother kissed her and went hurrying to her work.

Miriam ran and dabbled her hands in the clear water. She played with the flat pebbles and watched the distant fishing boats. Then suddenly she heard the sound of voices. They were coming towards the riverbank. She could see some young women led by one who was more beautiful than all the rest.

'She looks like a princess,' Miriam thought. But, oh! They were coming to the very place where her brother lay. Though frightened, Miriam crept nearer. She heard the beautiful one say to the waiting women, 'You may walk by the riverbank while I bathe. My maid will help me.'

Her maid nodded, and the others replied, 'We thank you, gracious daughter of almighty Pharaoh,' and walked away by the river.

'So she is a princess, an Egyptian princess,' Miriam murmured to herself. She knelt half-hidden by the reeds, and watched the princess dipping her feet into the cool water. But now she was pointing to something in the reeds. The basket! Pharaoh's daughter had seen the bulrush basket and was moving towards it. Miriam's heart began to pound as she saw the princess bending down.

'Come here!' the princess called to her maid. 'What can this be?'

The maid lifted the basket out of the water and placed it on the riverbank. Miriam came as close as she dared, watching, while the princess gazed into the basket. The baby cried and cried. Miriam saw the face of Pharaoh's daughter soften with pity.

'This is one of the Hebrews' children,' she said.

In a flash Miriam sprang forward. 'Shall I go and get a nurse from the Hebrew women so that she may nurse the child for you?' she asked breathlessly.

The maid looked in astonishment, but the princess turned, calmly saying, 'Yes, go!'

Miriam flew back home and poured out her story to her startled mother. Together they returned to the baby and Pharaoh's daughter.

'Take this infant away,' the princess commanded. 'Nurse it for me, and I will pay you.'

The baby was placed in his mother's arms, and she and Miriam hurried home. Once indoors, Mother turned to her daughter and gave her a big hug.

'What a sensible girl you are!' she cried, smiling all over her face. 'Now your baby brother is safe, for Pharaoh's daughter will protect him.'

Indeed, the baby grew up strong and well, to become the leader, Moses, chosen by the Lord God to save his people. But Miriam played her part too, didn't she? When she watched over the baby boy in the bulrush basket, and proved herself beyond doubt a most sensible sister.

Margaret Gregory

Exodus abridged

This sketch needs some careful presentation and a number of props, but the end result is well worth the effort.

Bible reference

Exodus 7 – 15

Cast

Narrator, Pharaoh, Moses, Aaron

Sorcerers and Magicians/Israelites (played by one person)

Plague-maker – technical person to facilitate plagues

Props

Drinking glass

Water in bottle or jug

Red food colouring

Table-tennis (ping-pong) balls

Red and black pens (to make 'boils' on Pharaoh)

Farmyard soft toys, such as sheep, cows and chickens
Crisp containers (such as Pringles) filled with seeds and sealed with sticky tape
Tambourine (optional)
Sign for sorcerers and magicians/Israelites

Narrator	Welcome once again to the Bible! Today we're going to hear about what happened in the book of Exodus, chapters 7 to 15. But before we begin, let's have a big round of applause for the one, the only, God's reluctant servant Moses! Now please welcome Moses' equally talented brother, Aaron! And now, introducing our special guest, God's chosen people. Let's hear it for the Israelites! Now, introducing that somewhat mysterious bunch, Pharaoh's sorcerers and magicians. And finally, you may remember this dastardly villain, whom God uses to show himself in a big way, the hard-hearted Pharaoh! Our story begins with Moses appearing before Pharaoh, and Pharaoh asking for a miracle.
Pharaoh	Let's have a miracle then.
Narrator	So Aaron threw down his stick and it turned into a snake.
	(*Aaron throws imaginary stick down, plague-maker makes hissing sounds.*)
Pharaoh	Cool!
Narrator	But Pharaoh wasn't impressed with Moses when his sorcerers and magicians did the same thing. (*Sorcerer and Magician steps forward smugly, waves and bows, then steps back.*)
Pharaoh	I'm not impressed.
Narrator	This was because Pharaoh's heart was hardened. So Moses said to Pharaoh:
Moses	God says, 'Let my people go, so that they can go into the desert and worship me. And so that you know I mean business, I'm gonna send a plague! A plague of blood.'
Pharaoh	Eh? What's that? A plate of bugs?
Moses	No, a plague of blood.
Pharaoh	Oh. (*Pause*) What's a plague of blood?
Moses	It's where all the water in the land, including the Nile river, your swimming pool and even your toilet, turns into blood, and stinks like crazy.

Pharaoh	Oh.
Narrator	And that's exactly what God did.
Pharaoh	(*Plague-maker pours clear water into glass with food colouring and hands to Pharaoh. Pharaoh smells the water and is repulsed*) Yuck!
Narrator	So Pharaoh said to Moses:
Pharaoh	OK, you can go.
Narrator	But Pharaoh wasn't impressed with Moses when his sorcerers and magicians did the same thing. (*Sorcerer and Magician steps forward again, waves and bows, then steps back.*)
Pharaoh	I'm not impressed.
Narrator	And Pharaoh changed his mind.
Pharaoh	I've changed my mind.
Narrator	This was because Pharaoh's heart was hardened. And so Moses said:
Moses	Let my people go! And so that you know I mean business, I'm gonna send a plague! A plague of frogs!
Pharaoh	Eh? What's that? A crate of dogs?
Moses	No, a plague of frogs.
Pharaoh	Oh. (*Pauses*) What's a plague of frogs?
Moses	It's where gazillions of frogs pop up out of the Nile river and go everywhere. They'll cover your garden, your house, your granny, and they'll even crawl into bed with you.
Pharaoh	Oh.
Narrator	And that's exactly what happened.
Pharaoh	(*Plague-maker starts to make 'ribbet' sounds*) Yuck! Moses, pray for me! Make these frogs go away!
Narrator	Moses did pray, and the frogs died. So Pharaoh said to Moses:
Pharaoh	OK, you can go.
Narrator	But Pharaoh wasn't impressed with Moses when his sorcerers and magicians did the same thing. (*Sorcerer and Magician repeats, same as above.*)
Pharaoh	I'm not impressed.
Narrator	And so Pharaoh changed his mind.

Pharaoh	I've changed my mind.
Narrator	This was because Pharaoh's heart was hardened. Then God told Moses to tell Aaron to stretch out his stick and hit the ground really hard, and the dust that came up would turn into gnats.
Pharaoh	Eh? What's that? Bats?
Narrator **Moses** **Aaron** }	GNATS!
Pharaoh	Oh.

(Aaron mimes this and Pharaoh starts to swat at imaginary gnats on his body.)

Narrator	And when Pharaoh's sorcerers and magicians tried to do the same thing (*Sorcerer and Magician step forward*), they found they could not. (*Sorcerer and Magician step back in shame.*) So they said to Pharaoh . . .
Sorcerer **and** **Magician** }	Only God can do that.
Narrator	But Pharaoh still wasn't impressed.
Pharaoh	I'm still not impressed.
Narrator	And this was because (*try to get audience to say it too*) Pharaoh's heart was hardened. So Moses kept on saying to Pharaoh:
Moses	Let my people go.
Narrator	And Pharaoh kept saying:
Pharaoh	No.
Narrator	So God, through Moses, sent a plague of. . .
Moses	Flies!

(Plague-maker starts making buzzing sounds, Pharaoh starts swatting at the air around him.)

Pharaoh	Yuck!
Narrator	Then God sent a plague of death on . . .
Moses	Livestock. You know, sheep and cows and chickens and things.

(Plague-maker throws soft toys at Pharaoh.)

Pharaoh	Yuck!
Narrator	Then God sent a plague of . . .
Moses	Boils!
Pharaoh	Eh? (*Hoping this time that he really has misheard*) What's that? Boils?

Moses and Narrator } Yep.

Pharaoh	Oh, no! (*Pulls up his sleeve to reveal drawn-on 'boils'*) Yuck!

Moses and Narrator } Yep.

Narrator	But throughout all these plagues, absolutely nothing happened to the Israelites, even though they were living in the same place.
Israelites	Really?
Narrator	Yep.
Israelites	Cool!
Narrator	Yep. And Moses kept on saying to Pharaoh:
Moses	Let my people go!
Narrator	And Pharaoh kept on saying:
Pharaoh	No!
Narrator	So God, through Moses, sent a plague of . . .
Moses	Hail. (*Throw ping-pong balls.*)
Pharaoh	Ouch!
Narrator	Then sent a plague of . . .
Moses	Locusts.
Pharaoh	What are locusts?
Moses	Insects that hop around and eat and destroy all your plants and trees and food and stuff.
Pharaoh	Oh. (*Pauses, locust sounds start*) Oh no!

Narrator Israelites Moses, etc. } Yep.

Narrator	And then God sent a plague of . . .
Moses	Darkness!
Narrator	And the darkness was so dark, you could FEEL it! And it lasted for three days.
Pharaoh	(*Starts to feel around as if blind*) I can't see!
Israelites	I can! Na na na na na!
Moses	This is happening because you won't let us go.
Pharaoh	(*Groans*) Oooh . . . OK, you can go.
Narrator	But Pharaoh changed his mind.
Pharaoh	I've changed my mind.
Narrator	And all this was because Pharaoh's heart was hardened. So God sent one more plague. He sent an angel to pass over all of Egypt and kill all the firstborn, even the cows' and sheep's firstborn.
Pharaoh **Moses,** **etc.**	Oh no!
Narrator	But God told the Israelites to make a special meal with lamb and flatbread that night. He told the Israelites to put the blood of that lamb on the outsides of their doors so that the angel would know to leave the houses that belonged to the Israelites alone and not to kill their oldest children.
Moses **and** **Aaron**	Phew!
Narrator	But Pharaoh didn't put lamb's blood on his door, and his oldest son died that very night, along with all the other firstborn in the land. And Pharaoh was very sad. So he said to Moses and Aaron:
Pharaoh	Go away into the desert and worship your God! Just stop all these plagues and leave us alone.
Narrator	And that's exactly what they did. The Israelites took everything they had, their animals, their clothes, their food, and they left Egypt as fast as they could. Their Egyptian neighbours even gave them silver and gold and helped them to leave. They went and camped in the desert and the Lord God looked after them. But suddenly, Pharaoh changed his mind.
Pharaoh	I've changed my mind.

Narrator	He decided he wanted the Israelites back to be his slaves again. So he got all his horses and soldiers together and ran after Moses and the Israelites as fast as he could. And the Israelites got scared.
Israelites	We're scared!
Narrator	But Moses said:
Moses	Don't be afraid. Just wait and watch out. The Lord God is going to fight for us.
Narrator	That's exactly what God did. God told Moses to hold up his stick over the Red Sea, just in front of them (*Moses does this as the narrator speaks*). As Moses raised his stick, God split the sea in half and created dry ground for the Israelites to walk on so that they could escape from the Egyptians. Now when the Israelites saw all this, they were seriously impressed.
Israelites	We're seriously impressed!
Narrator	But they were even more impressed when God closed the Red Sea and swallowed up all of Pharaoh's soldiers and horses.
Israelites	Whey hey!
Pharaoh	(*Terrified*) AHHH!
	(*Exits running.*)
Narrator	So God led Moses, Aaron and the Israelites on to a couple of scenic spots called Marah and Elim where they camped and rested.
Israelites	(*Contented*) Ahhh!
Narrator	Now, God had promised the Israelites that he would bring them out of Egypt and into freedom. That's exactly what he did. So, to celebrate, Moses and a woman called Miriam did a little song and dance.
Moses **Aaron** **Israelites** **Narrator** }	(*Picking up tambourines*) 'When the Spirit of the Lord is within my heart' (SHF 604) (*All the characters except Pharaoh exit singing and dancing.*)

Barbara Hastings Cox

41

Joshua

The long march

How can you tell the story of the fall of Jericho without a huge cast, trumpets, military uniforms and a large wall? This sketch provides the answer by focusing upon two members of the Israelite army as they trudge around the city walls.

Bible reference
Joshua 6

Cast
Man 1, Man 2

Man 1   Walk, walk, walk. All we ever do in this army is march.

Man 2   Stop complaining. It's better than fighting. You don't often hear of soldiers getting killed walking, do you?

Man 1   I wouldn't mind, but we aren't even going anywhere. I enjoy a good walk with the dog as much as anyone. But not this boring walk, walk, walk.

Man 2   Stop complaining. The officers say this is the last day on this march.

Man 1   I jolly well hope so. We've been walking round and round for six days now, always on the same route. Today it must be five or six times already. I've lost count. What is there to count on anyway? It all looks the same. My feet are killing me.

Man 2   Better to have your feet kill you than someone's sword. Shut up and march.

Man 1   Walk, walk, walk. Do you know, we could have walked all the way back to Egypt by now. My dad always used to say things were not that bad in Egypt. Hard work there was, but at least there was no army – and NO WALKING. I don't know why we didn't stay there. If it hadn't been for that Moses fellow we would be quite comfortable now, just like my dad said. He was all in favour of turning back some forty years or so ago now. Pity he died in the desert. Quite a leader was my dad you know.

Man 2   Your dad was a rebel, not a leader. If people like him had not complained and argued so much we would have settled down years ago, and not spent all that time in the desert. You should be careful with your talk of turning back. There have been too many disasters caused by that kind of talk already and you may be overheard.

Man 1   Who can hear us? Only the other soldiers, and look at them. They are as fed up as I am. What will they report? That one of the men is fed up with walking? We're ALL fed up with the whole business. Promised land. What promised land? Have you seen any milk and honey lately?

Moses and all his promises. Fat lot of good they were. What happened to him? Died just before we got here. Probably knew it was all a lie.

Man 2 Aren't you ever satisfied? Didn't you marvel at the way we crossed the river back there? On dry land. Have you ever seen a river dry up before, just to let people through? No, I believe that what Moses said was true. That God is on our side, and this really is the promised land. So just you watch what you're saying. It wouldn't be the first time that doubts have led to riots, and riots have resulted in some kind of disaster.

(Pause.)

Man 1 As I said just now, who's going to listen to us? Will those people crowded on top of that city wall listen? No, they only come every day to watch us mugs. I bet they wonder what we're up to. They must think we're daft. *(Pause)* Well that makes one more lap, I think.

Man 2 Six today I make it, or is it five? Anyway, Joshua did say that the trumpets will blow on the last time around. Then we all shout and the walls of that great city will fall down. So long as he is keeping count I don't suppose it matters. He's a good leader you know. Took over well from Moses. He does what God tells him to do and then God makes it all happen. Better than people like your old dad, always arguing and disobeying God.

Man 1 Don't start on my dad again. He wasn't that bad. He just didn't like to be the odd one out, that's all. So he went along with the crowd. No harm in that, is there? Why try to be different anyway? It's much easier to follow the crowd, do what everybody else does.

Man 2 Depends on what the crowd is doing. If you really know that what the crowd does is wrong, then why follow them? Take that crowd on the city wall. Every day they all come to stare at us, trying to find out what we're up to. Just a crowd all doing the same thing all the time. According to Joshua, by this time tomorrow they'll all be dead. How's that for all doing the same thing, being part of the crowd? Not so good, is it, when you put it like that?

Man 1 Suppose not.

Man 2 Like all our fathers who died in the desert. They all wanted to do the same thing, the very thing you wanted to do just now. Hot foot it back to Egypt and slavery as soon as things got a little tough. Sometimes freedom has to be fought for. Sometimes it's hard work.

Man 1 Every day those people come and stand on the wall and stare at us. They really must think we're stupid or something. A whole army just walking around the massive fortifications they've built.

Man 2 If Joshua says to march, then that's good enough for me. God must have told him of a plan to make the walls fall down. If it's God's plan, we'd better follow it.

(*Pause.*)

Man 1 Walk, walk, walk . . . Do you know, I just had a thought? If those rotten walls fell down right now then most of those people staring at us would be killed. Serves them right for being so nosey. Perhaps everybody in the city is crowded on that wall, looking down at us. They would all be killed, without us having to fight at all. Perhaps that's just as well. With all this walking I don't feel much like fighting anyway.

Man 2 Save your breath for shouting . . . I think I can hear the trumpets starting . . .

Robert Cuin

Samuel

The boy who woke in the night

A lyrical version of the story of the boy Samuel. A group of children could listen to it with eyes closed so that they can imagine the scene without interruption. Used like this, it could lead into a time of silent prayer. Or it could fuel an interesting discussion about hearing God's voice today.

Bible reference

1 Samuel 2.18 – 3.21

Samuel didn't live at home like most children. He stayed in the temple at a place called Shiloh.

It happened like this. Samuel's mother, who was called Hannah, had once longed, and longed, for a baby of her own. She promised God that, if she ever had a little son, she wouldn't keep him for herself. She would let him serve and worship the Lord God in his house.

At last God granted her wish, and so it was that Samuel lived in the temple with Eli, the priest.

Now today Samuel had a very special treat, because his father and mother were coming to visit him. Early in the morning, Samuel opened the temple doors, and there they were already waiting for him. 'How you've grown, Samuel!' cried his mother, giving him a huge hug. 'I do hope the coat I've made will fit.' Once they were in the temple she slipped the coat over the linen tunic Samuel always wore and stepped back. 'What do you think, Father?' 'Perfect!' he said, smiling.

Samuel ran to show Eli his fine new coat. But he was soon back with his father and mother, for all too soon it would be time to say goodbye, and then it would be another long year before they returned.

Samuel was always sad to see his parents go. But at the same time he was happy to remain in the temple, helping Eli to serve the Lord. The old man was like a second father to him, though Eli himself had two grown sons of his own. But they were very wicked men, and took no notice of Eli at all. So it was good that young Samuel was there to help and comfort him.

As Eli grew older, and his eyes became weaker, he needed Samuel more than ever. One night Samuel settled down to sleep in his special place in the temple. A lamp was still burning and Eli was not far away.

Suddenly Samuel woke up – a voice was calling his name. 'Eli,' he thought, 'it must be Eli.' Samuel called back, 'I'm here.' He jumped up and ran over to him. 'Here I am, you called me.' The old man murmured, 'I didn't call. Lie down again, boy!'

Samuel did so and went back to sleep. But in a short while the voice called again, 'Samuel!' He sat bolt upright. 'I'm here!' This time it had to be Eli and Samuel ran to his side. 'No I didn't call,' the old man repeated. 'Go and lie down, I tell you.' Then it happened once more. The voice calling his name, and Samuel replying, 'I'm here!' But when he came to Eli this time, the old man sat up and looked at the boy thoughtfully.

'I didn't call your name, Samuel. What you heard was the voice of the Lord God.' He went on, 'If he calls your name again, you must answer, "Speak Lord, for your servant is listening." '

So Samuel lay down in the shadows, waiting and listening. He couldn't sleep. The Lord came and stood close by, calling, 'Samuel! Samuel!' The boy remembered exactly what Eli had told him and said, 'Speak Lord, for your servant is listening.'

And the Lord God spoke, saying that nothing could make him forget or forgive the wickedness of Eli's sons. These sons had to be punished, and through them, the father, who had done so little to curb their evil ways. The next morning Samuel got up and opened the temple doors. He was frightened about giving Eli the Lord's message, and wished very much that he didn't have to tell him. But soon Eli called Samuel to him. He insisted on hearing everything that the Lord God had said about Eli's wicked sons and the punishment they would receive.

It was hard for Eli to bear, but Samuel was still there to help and comfort him. And though Samuel grew up to become a great man, Surely he never forgot Eli – nor the night when he woke, to hear God's voice calling his name.

Margaret Gregory

David

Giants cannot do everything

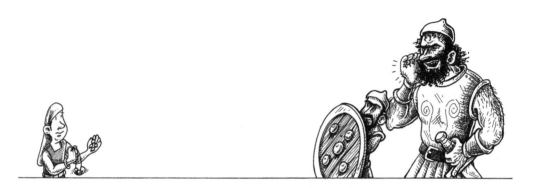

Goliath's parents are proud of their strong son. Children will enjoy this story which comes from such an unexpected perspective.

Bible reference
1 Samuel 17

'What a fine baby!' cried the midwife to the mother.

He was certainly huge and hairy. As if to stress the fact, he clenched his little fists and kicked vigorously so that he nearly fell out of her arms. 'Big G' was the nick-name given to him by his father, who was in the Philistine army fighting the Israelites.

'This boy of mine is going to be the greatest soldier ever,' he boasted to everyone. 'You wait till he grows up.'

Big G was thoroughly spoilt by his mother and sisters and as he grew up he became the leader of the boys in the camp. Being so strong he could beat them in throwing the spear and wrestling and he could run many kilometres without tiring. When he worshipped in the temple of the god Dagon, he stood head and shoulders above everyone there. When he finally became a soldier he told his father, 'I'll squash those invading Israelites like flies when we go to war.'

By now Big G was three metres tall, so he had to sleep in a special tent large enough to make sure his feet did not stick out beneath the goats' hair covering. His snoring was enough to wake the dead, so he slept apart from his comrades. His armour of bronze weighed sixty-four kilograms. He had a helmet to protect his head, a breastplate for his chest and even protective armour on his legs. His spear weighed six kilograms and its shaft was as heavy as the beam of a weaver's loom. He had a man to carry his heavy shield before him.

'This is our land, my son,' said his father. 'It's all because King Saul of Israel wants it that the lord of our city goes to war. I hear that the king is mad and has to have a shepherd boy play the harp to him to soothe his rages.'

'I know. His name is David and he has killed a lion and a bear with his hands while minding the sheep. I could kill a hundred lions and bears with *my* hands,' said Big G, clenching his huge fists until his face grew red with the effort.

War came and the armies of the Philistines and Israelites faced each other across the plain of Gaza. The Philistines stood massed on one mountainside and the Israelites on the other. Big G was sent out from the camp of the Philistines as champion to cry out, 'Won't you come out to battle, you slaves of Saul? I am the greatest! Choose a man to meet me. If he can kill me in a fair fight, we will become your slaves. But if I prove too strong for him, and kill him, you shall be our slaves and serve us. I defy you to send out a man to beat me.'

For forty days, both in the morning and the evening, Big G shouted out his challenge. And no one in the Israelite army took it up, for they ran from him in fear whenever the bright sun glanced off his bronze helmet and they saw the size of the man they would have to fight.

'We've got them! We'll slay them!' shouted Big G at the end of forty days, and the battle lines were drawn up for the conflict that was to take place the next day.

But before the fight began, a rumour ran round the Philistine camp that a challenger had been found. He was none other than David, the shepherd boy who had been sent by his father to bring food to his soldier brothers in the camp.

'A shepherd boy!' sneered Big G. 'I'll shear him like one of his own sheep and tie him up in his own harp strings.'

'He can scarcely stagger under the armour King Saul has put on him,' laughed his father. 'You'll be able to step on him as if he were a scorpion without a sting.'

The next day Big G, fully armed, walked proudly down to the valley in front of the massed armies, with his shield-bearer going before him. He looked

contemptuously down at David, dressed only in a tunic and headcloth and carrying no spear. He was holding his shepherd's crook, a sling and the pouch round his waist that usually held his food for the day. David saw the look and trembled for an instant as the Philistine shouted, 'Am I a dog that you come out against me with sticks? I swear by the name of Dagon that I'll give your flesh to the birds and the beasts.'

David tilted his head right back to look at his enemy. He shouted in return, 'You have come against me with spear and dagger. But I come against you in the name of the Lord of hosts, the God of the army of Israel, whom you have defied. The Lord will put you into my power this day and I will kill you so that all the world shall know that there is a God in Israel.'

Big G laughed as he held high his sword and rushed upon the small figure defying him. The noise of his feet thundered on the ground. David calmly drew a pebble from his pouch, placed it skilfully in his sling and whirled it about his head before letting fly. It struck Goliath on the right temple with great force. There was a mighty crash as the giant fell to the ground and lay still. At once, David ran to him, seized the sword and cut off the huge head. He raised his arms in triumph.

'The battle is the Lord's!' he cried. And all the Philistines turned and fled.

Sheila Forsdyke

A rat in a trap

After fighting Goliath, David went on to more military successes. Eventually King Saul became dangerously jealous and David escaped into exile. This sketch, with a small cast of four, captures the bizarre moment when David had the opportunity for revenge in a one-man coup.

Bible reference

1 Samuel 24

Cast

Saul, Guards 1 and 2, David

Props

Robe and a piece of cloth

(King Saul and two of his guards are walking in the desert.)

Guard 1   What's wrong, Saul? You don't seem at all happy today.

Guard 2   Yes, you've just won another battle against the Philistines, and still you're not happy.

Saul   I hate the desert. It's too hot and I'm tired and thirsty.

Guard 1   Then why not give up and go home? You don't imagine that we enjoy it too much. I could do with a drink and a lie down right now.

Saul   I can't give up now. Not until I've caught that David and killed him.

Guard 1   I can't think why you want to kill him. When has he ever done anything to you?

Guard 2   Yes, all I can remember is that it was you who invited David to the palace in the first place. You wanted somebody to play the harp whenever you felt depressed. What happened? Don't you like harp music any more? Me, I can't stand the thing.

Guard 1   If you've gone off music, why not ask him to stop playing – or simply to leave? No point in killing a guy just because you don't like his music any more.

Saul   No, you idiots, it's not the music. I still like that. It's just that the young upstart now wants to become king in place of me and I can't allow that.

Guard 2   I don't remember David ever saying that he wanted to be king. Though, come to think of it, I did hear of Samuel going to see his father once on some secret mission. But isn't that just a rumour that's got around?

Saul   Well – all right. Perhaps it's not David himself then, but the people who want to make him king. It really gets to me how the people keep reminding me about that Goliath affair.

Guard 1   Oh yeah, I remember him, massive guy, biggest I ever saw. I never thought David would win . . . not with just a sling and a few rocks.

Saul   Well if David just disappears – dead like – then the people can't make him king after all and I can stay where I am. And if I stay where I am, then it's good jobs for you two – get it ?

Guard 1   Well I don't like it – he was a good friend of your own son.

Saul   Yes and that boy of mine helped him to escape. Now it's up to us to find him and quietly get rid of him. News is that he's somewhere in this desert, and that's why we're here.

Guard 1   Well . . . if the people want to make David king, surely they will do it in the city, not in the desert. I say let's head back home and catch him in the town. I could probably get a drink and a good night's rest first.

Saul   You be careful. There are plenty more men in the army who would be glad of your position, you know. Now you two keep watch. I am just going into this cave for a minute.

Guard 1   Whatever for?

Saul	Don't ask – it's private. When you've got to go then you've got to go. Just you two keep a look out, that's all.

(*Saul goes into the cave and the two guards remain outside.*)

Guard 1	Should have gone before he came out. That's what my mother always said.
Guard 2	You should be careful of what you say. You know how often he gets angry. We can't afford to upset him.
Guard 1	Well, I feel sorry for David. He's never hurt anybody, apart from Philistines, and nobody likes Philistines. He should be a national hero but all Saul is doing is having us and half the army chasing him around this desert like a wild animal. I like the lad and I can't help feeling sorry for him, that's all.
Guard 2	I know, but Saul has a point. The people want David to be king instead. Do you want that? You'll lose your top position in the army.
Guard 1	I could live with that. At least I wouldn't be spending half my life in this miserable desert. You know what I think? I think that David should never have come to the palace. You heard what happened the other week?
Guard 2	The spear incident, you mean?
Guard 1	Yes, that's the one. Good job old Saul was in such a rage. His aim is normally much better than that!
Guard 2	Shhh . . . He's coming back.

(*Saul reappears.*)

Saul	That's better. Now let's go and find my enemy and his merry men.
Guard 2	Hey, Saul, what happened to your cloak? Did you tear it or something in that cave?
Guard 1	Here, let me have a look . . . It's not torn, it's cut. A piece has been cut right off. You didn't slip on your sword by any chance and cut your own coat?
Saul	Now he accuses me of being incompetent. I do not slip and fall on my sword and cut my clothes. I am not some stupid guard, you know. I am the KING!
David	(*Calls out in a loud voice*) Your Majesty – King Saul!

(*Saul turns around to see David standing there. David bows down to the king.*)

David   Why do you only listen to the people who say that I am trying to harm you? Do you recognize this?

Saul   That's the piece off my robe. How did you get it?

David   Just now, in that cave. You didn't know that I was hiding in there and the Lord put you right into my hands. Some of my men wanted me to kill you, but I felt sorry for you, and would not hurt you. After all, you are the king, chosen by God.

Guard 2   Do you want me to go over there and kill him for you right now?

David   I hope that this piece of your robe that I cut off will convince you that I do not want to kill you. But you are hunting me down to kill me. Why are you doing this? May the Lord judge which one of us is wrong. May he punish you for your actions against me, for I will not harm you in the least.

Guard 2   I could kill him if you like.

Saul   No wait, let's hear what else he has to say. David, is that really you? David, my son?

David   Evil is always done by evil men. I won't hurt you even though you're trying to kill me. Look at what the king of Israel is up to – he is chasing me, and what am I? A flea or even a dead dog!

Guard 2   You sure you don't want me to kill him now?

Saul   Oh shut up!

David   The Lord will judge between us. He will save me from you. He will look into the matter and decide which one of us is right and which one is wrong.

Saul   I know that you're right and I'm wrong. You've been good to me, while I've only done you wrong. Today you've shown me how good you are because you did not kill me, though the Lord put me into your hands. How often does a man catch his enemy and then let him go unharmed? The Lord bless you for what you have done today.

(David disappears into the desert. Saul is again alone with his two guards.)

Guard 2   Shall we go after him now, sir, and kill him for you?

Saul   No. Leave him alone. You know, I'm sure that he will one day become the king of Israel. Let's go home. There is nothing else for us to do here.

Guard 1   Yes, let's go home. I don't like the desert.

Guard 2 Perhaps peace is better than war. Well at least it is easier – for a guard, that is.

Guard 1 I can't make you out. One minute all you want to do is kill somebody. Now all you want to do is to go home.

Saul Will you two just shut up! I'm having a bad day!

Robert Cuin

David the poet king

A poem for older children to ponder in exploring the story of David.

Bible reference

1 and 2 Samuel

Jesse's son, the shepherd king,
grew up protecting sheep,
thought his father's business interests
were more crucial than his sleep.
So he learnt the hard way how to save
his flock from lions and bears,
and was not afraid to act in faith
to back up urgent prayers.

David was a soldier king
with many enemies
who were jealous of the wealth and fame
he'd earned in victories,
which had made him seem invincible,
but David knew the score:
while his glory was a fading flower,
God reigns for evermore.

David was a poet king
who told it like it is.
His words were never padded out
with self-indulgent fizz.
He revealed to us in detail
just how evil fleeced his heart,
and that only God could save him
to give muscle to his art.

Peter Comaish

Psalms

All-age service

A short outline for a teaching service about King David. It could well be used as the first part of a family communion service.

Welcome

Sentence   'My soul will rejoice in the Lord, and delight in his salvation' (Psalm 35. 9).

Introduction   Today we are going to think about King David. We are going to think about three ways that he prayed, and we are going to try to do them too.

Hymn   'Come let us join our cheerful songs, with angels round the throne' (HTC 206)

Talk 1   The first kind of prayer of David's we are going to think about is the way that he worshipped God.

Ask for two volunteers to help you tell the story. Dress Michal in a robe, and give David a crown. Your volunteers can act as much or as little as they like. Retell the story from 2 Samuel 6. 12b – 6.20-23. This is not the time to explain the ark of the covenant, just talk about a special procession. The main thing to bring out is David's wholehearted worship, compared with Michal's attitude.

We too can worship God wholeheartedly. Let's have a go in this song about David.

Song   'When the Spirit of the Lord is within my heart, I will dance as David danced' (SHF 604)

Reading   Psalm 35.1-8 (*The anger and passion needs to show in this reading.*)

Talk 2   The second thing that David knew about prayer was that he could pray about anything and everything, however he felt. Let's try and show each other some different feelings with our faces. (*Ask people to turn to the person next to them, and do a happy face. Then a sad one, and so on. End with an angry face.*) Sometimes we think that we have to be feeling good before we can talk to God. That's not true. God is not surprised when we are bitter and angry, and he is the best person to tell all about it, just like David did.

Prayer   Now we're going to have a chance to be like David again, and tell God about the things that make us angry. First let's close our eyes. Now, think about that person or thing that makes you feel cross or angry. Curl up your hands very tight to show how angry you feel. In a couple of minutes of quiet, tell God, just inside your head, how you feel. Now, if you want to, open your hands to show that you have started to let God into that thing that makes you so cross.

Song   'You are my hiding place' (SHF 629)

Reading   Psalm 51.1-12 (*David's sorrow needs to show in this reading.*)

Talk 3   The last thing we are going to learn about David is that he knew just what to pray when he had done something wrong. Just like all of us, David could be selfish and horrible. The words we have just heard were written by David after a time when he had done something *very* wrong. When he realized how bad he had been, he knew just what to do. He went and said sorry to God. He didn't try to pretend he hadn't done anything. He told God straight away how sorry he was.

Prayer   We need to say sorry to God for things too. Let's close our eyes to pray. (*These prayers could be printed out, or put on an OHP acetate.*)

Dear God,
We are so sorry for the times when we hurt you, and other people.
We are sorry
We are so sorry for the times when we are selfish.
We are sorry
We are so sorry for the times when we won't forgive people.
We are sorry
We are so sorry for the times we forget how much you love us.
We are sorry

Thank you, Lord, that you always forgive us, and make us clean again when we come to you and say sorry. We pray in the name of Jesus,
Amen.

Please help us, Lord, to be like David.
Help us to worship and love you with all our heart, mind, soul and strength.
Help us to tell you all about the things that make us angry and unhappy.
Help us to say sorry when we have done wrong.
Amen.

We pray for all people who are living in situations that are unfair:
For those who have not enough food,

For those who do not have good shelter,
For those who have no hope.
Please, Lord, meet their needs, and help us to live our lives
in service to you and others.
Amen.

The Lord's Prayer

Offertory hymn   'All people that on earth do dwell' (HTC 14)

The blessing

Jean Ball

Daniel

The story of Daniel

This song about Daniel should be sung to the tune of Davy Crockett. It could also be a rap or chant, or a presentation in itself with different parts played, including a town crier.

Bible reference

Daniel 6

Once upon a time, King Darius said,
'This is my decree and it shall be read,
"For thirty days prayer to me alone shall be said,
And those who disobey to the lions shall be fed." '

Daniel, don't pray, Daniel,
They'll throw you in the lions' den.

Daniel loved his king, but he loved God more,
He prayed by the window and ignored the law.
He prayed every day and the king's men saw,
And they put him in the den and shut the door.

Daniel, oh dear Daniel,
They've put him in the lions' den.

Daniel went in and the lions roared,
But straight from heaven came an angel of the Lord
Who whispered to the lions and with one accord
They settled on the ground where they slumbered and they snored.

Daniel, God bless Daniel,
He's walked from the lions' den.

The moral of the story is that if faith is true,
There's nothing in the world that God cannot do,
The Lord loves you now just like Daniel then.
Daniel walked from the lions' den.

Dorothy Morris

Jonah

Celebrating Jonah

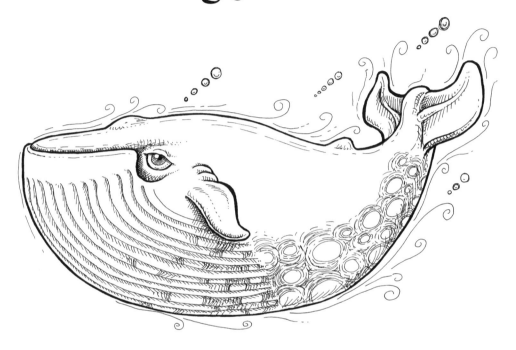

Bible reference

Jonah

Sing some songs as people arrive, especially any songs with a seaside theme.

Welcome   We have come together to sing God's praises and to worship him, and as we do so today, we shall be celebrating the story of Jonah, God's reluctant prophet. God calls each one of us to be his messengers so that the world may hear and turn to him. Let all creation join in declaring the wonderful love of God.

Praise   Sing to the Lord a new song,

For he has done marvellous things.

Sing for joy, all the earth,

Praise him with songs and shouts of joy.

Hymn   'Jesus shall reign' (HTC 516)

Dramatized reading   *Ask the congregation to help you with the telling of the story by producing sound effects. Practise with them the sounds of wind, waves, rain, thunder and so on, using voices, whistles, hands and feet.*

Using The Dramatised Bible *(p. 800), read* Jonah 1, *with the congregation making storm noises at appropriate moments (verses 4, 11, 12, 13), then suddenly becoming calm at verse 15. You could even have the captain and sailors in suitable nautical dress, and Jonah looking rather shifty with dark glasses and a travelling bag. Depending on how ambitious your readers/actors are, they may be able to ham up or act out the story, especially the last bit where Jonah goes overboard.*

Hymn or song   'Will your anchor hold in the storms of life?' (HON 561);   'Wide, wide as the ocean' (JP 292)

Talk   *Talk about how horrible it would be to be swallowed by a large fish.* Think of the smell inside. Could you breathe? What else would be in there? Has anyone here ever been eaten? Probably not, but no doubt some members of the congregation have been in some pretty bad scrapes. Would anyone be willing to describe briefly any dramatic experiences they have had with animals, or in the sea?

You don't have to have been in a scrape like that to feel like Jonah sometimes. Let's read together his prayer from inside the belly of the big fish.

Prayer   *The congregation reads out, from the service sheet, the words of Jonah's prayer, in* Jonah 2.

Then reveal to the congregation a large card or board at the front of the church with the outline of a huge fish upon it. Have lots of 'scales' ready to stick onto the fish. Invite people, in groups of two or three, to write onto their scale a prayer for someone or some group of people in distress. Stick the prayers onto the fish as they are done. When they are all completed, read them out, connecting them together with the response:

In their distress they call to you,

Lord, hear your children's cry.

Song   'Come, listen to my tale' (JP 30)

The end of the story   *Explain that Jonah did now obey God's call, but there were still some lessons to be learned. You could either tell the story in your own words, or continue with* The Dramatised Bible *with Jonah 3 and 4 (pp. 802–3).*

Song   'Colours of day' (JP 28)

Talk   *Mention the fact that the story of Jonah is told in the Bible like a cartoon, with its vivid images illustrating both the humiliating and the heroic in Jonah and his fellow travellers.*

A wry humour runs through the tale from beginning to end. Did Jonah ever come to laugh at himself? Certainly one of the funniest bits often gets overlooked. This is the extraordinary image of the sheep and cattle fasting and wearing sackcloth. The relationship between humans and animals in this story suggests more even than this: that God's love for all his creatures should make us live more gently on his earth.

Coming back to people instead of animals, the story also suggests people should be given every opportunity to respond to God. Often it is the messenger himself who is the problem, just like Jonah. The 'sign of Jonah' of which Jesus spoke is, yes, about the need for all to repent and have faith, but also about the fact that it was to save and not to judge that Jesus came.

We may at times refuse God's call, like Jonah did at first, but more often perhaps we claim to be doing his work yet still fail to grasp the enormous scope of his gracious purpose. We may need to look well beyond the boundaries of church as we know it to see what God is doing out there. Let us aim to be willing messengers, with a big vision of God's good purposes.

Prayer

O Lord of earth and air and sky and sea,
hear us when we pray,
have mercy on us, and forgive us our sins.

When we hear your call, may we be ready to obey,
have mercy on us, and strengthen us to serve you.

When we are in distress, hear our prayer,
and let our cry come to you, O Lord.

May all people everywhere turn to you and to your love,
and may all creation sing your praise!

The Lord's Prayer

Hymn   'All creatures of our God and King' (HTC 13)
or 'Let all the world in every corner sing' (HTC 342)

The blessing

Malcolm Williams

THE NEW TESTAMENT

Christmas

Nativity for all ages

This service is based upon a traditional French nativity pageant. Each scene of the nativity is presented in a tableau form and, as there are no lines to be learned, small children can take a full part in the service.

The church should be darkened at the beginning of the service, the stage empty and screens or curtains hiding the manger.

Bible references

Isaiah 9.2-7 and 40.1-5

Luke 1.26-38 and 2.1-16

Luke 4.18-19 and 18.15-17

Revelation 7.14-17

Choir   First verse of 'O come, O come, Emmanuel' (HON 358). As lights increase the congregation joins in further verses.

(*Enter prophet.*)

Reading   With mime, adapted from either Isaiah 9.2,6,7, or Isaiah 40.1-5 and 9.

(*Exit prophet.*)

Choir   'How lovely on the mountains' (HON 219) or 'Hark! a herald voice is calling' (HON 196)

(*Enter Mary and kneels in prayer.*)

Reading   With mime, adapted from Luke 1.26-38.

(*Gabriel appears at verse 28 holding a white lily. He salutes Mary, who starts back amazed, but then listens quietly.*)

Choir   Either 'Angelus ad virginum' (CFC 6) or 'The holly and the ivy' (SNDBC 71)

(*During the singing, Gabriel leaves the lily by Mary and exits. Mary resumes prayer posture, then picks up the flower and looks at it thoughtfully. Exits.*)

All   'It came upon the midnight clear' (HAMNS 41) or 'Hark the glad sound! The Saviour comes' (HAMNS 30)

Reading   Luke 2.1-7

(*During the reading, Mary and Joseph make their way slowly to Bethlehem, where the innkeeper is persuaded to find room in the stable. The tableau forms behind the screens.*)

All   'O little town of Bethlehem' (HON 377) or 'Once in Royal David's city' (HON 403)

(*Screens are removed during carol. Shepherds enter stage front.*)

Reading   Luke 2.8-16 (or 20) with mime.

(*Angel appears and is joined by heavenly host at words 'and suddenly. . .'. Shepherds hasten to manger, kneel, then move to either side. Exit angels.*)

Choir   'Little Jesus sweetly sleep' (OBC 87)

All   'Go, tell it on the mountain' (HON 165)

(*Shepherds exit.*)

King's voice (*From back*)   Matthew 1.2

Soloist   'We three kings' (HON 537)

(*Procession of kings enters, with page boys optional, during solo.*)

All   'As with gladness' (HON 41)

(*Kings exit during carol.*)

Reading   Luke 4.18-19

(*Procession of Sorrows enters as music, e.g. Adagio by Albinoni, is played or a solo such as 'Come unto me' from the* Messiah *is sung. Two angels come front stage and remove the blind girl's bandage, beggars' bowls, crutches, slave-master's whip, etc. and touch the lepers. All react to their healing, run to the manger and bow. When all have gathered round . . .*)

All (*or choir*)   'All poor men and humble' (OBC 34)

(*Procession exits.*)

Reading   Luke 18.15-17

(*Procession of children – possibly in national costumes – enters while carols are sung.*)

All   'Girls and boys, leave your toys'(JP 344)

(*Some of the procession might put toys, baskets of fruit and so on, at the crib, then take tableau positions until all have knelt and looked at the baby.*)

Children   'Away in a manger' (HON 51)

All   'Infant holy, infant lowly' (HON 251)

(*Children exit during carol.*)

Reading   Revelation 7.9-12

All   'Hark, the herald-angels sing' (HON 199)

(*Procession of the faithful representing all nations and walks of life enters. They bow at manger, then take tableau positions.*)

Reading   Revelation 7.14-17

All   'O come, all ye faithful' (HON 357)

(*Procession exits during carol; the stage is quiet and still.*)

Choir   'Sing lullaby' (HON 445) or 'O little one sweet'(HON 376)

(*If lighting effect is possible, the shadow of a cross should overlie the manger during the carol. A quiet pause follows.*)

Prayers

John and Ruth Tiller

Big secret
An all-age Christmas talk

The aim of this talk is to create an awareness that the biggest secret of Christmas is that Jesus is the Son of God. It might be used as the talk in the 'Nativity for all ages' service.

Bible reference

Isaiah 9.5-6

Preparation

Fill a large bag (a pillow-case will do) with enough chocolate bars to ensure that every child present will receive one. Attach a large sheet of paper to both sides with the words 'Big secret'. Hang the bag up in a prominent position in the church with a cord long enough to allow you to lower it easily. Draw an OHP sheet of a pregnant woman (profile is probably best). Prepare a second OHP sheet with the text of a standard birth announcement (e.g. 'To Mr and Mrs X the birth of a baby son, X, on 3 May 1998'). Prepare a third OHP sheet with the text of Isaiah 9.6, putting the words 'To us . . .' in a different colour for emphasis. In fact after those two words I put in brackets the words 'That's everybody, folks!'

Presentation

Ask the children how many of them are good at keeping secrets and why it is so hard to keep them. Point out that there is a big secret in church today and ask whether anyone has seen it. Say that you will only tell them what that big secret is at the end of your talk and only if they listen to you.

Put up the OHP of the pregnant woman. Ask them what secret this woman has. Who had that kind of

secret at the first Christmas? Who else knew about Mary's secret? (Joseph, Gabriel, Elizabeth, God.) What is exciting about this kind of secret? (e.g. Will it be a boy or a girl; how heavy will the child be; what colour eyes; when will he/she arrive?) All of this, of course, Mary and Joseph found out on Christmas Day.

What do parents sometimes do when their baby is born? (They make an announcement in the papers.) Put up an OHP with the standard announcement. Then point out that the announcement of Jesus' birth was not in any newspaper. Can anyone guess where we can find it? (The Bible.) Say that you will show it to them and put up the OHP with the text from Isaiah. Draw attention to the words 'To us'. Jesus did not belong just to Mary and Joseph. He belongs to everyone. And that brings us to the biggest secret of all: Jesus was not just Mary's baby, he was God's baby. Jesus was the Son of God. Now that I have told you the secret about Jesus – that he is the Son of God – is there anything else you want to know. (A sea of hands should appear.) Ask them what they think is inside the bag. Lower it and hand out the chocolates either then or at the end of the service.

Paul Thomas

In the picture

Cast

Director, Lavinia, Photographer, Letitia, Nigel, Mary, Joseph, Father Christmas
and a number of 'extras' (who might be chosen on the day from the
congregation)

Props

A mixture of costumes for a traditional nativity play
(such as shepherds' costumes)

*(The photographer and director are on stage making final preparations for their Christmas
card shot. Enter Lavinia, with Mary, Joseph and the baby.)*

Director Thank you, Lavinia. Can you make sure no one disturbs us?

Lavinia	Sure thing, Mr de Mille.
Director	(*Watches Lavinia move to the side, then speaks to the photographer*) Finished?
Photographer	Cameras are OK. Floods fine. Spots great . . .
Director	Well, OK then. It's all yours. I don't see why they needed a director anyway. With these Christmas cards, all you need is the right subject matter. Not much to go wrong, is there?
Photographer	Close together please . . . facing each other a little more. Now, Mary, look at the child . . . great, that's it . . . a big smile for Christmas . . .
Director	No. Hang on a sec. I don't like it. It won't do. There's nothing happening. There's nothing to grab you. Why should anyone go for this picture?
Photographer	Simplicity.
Director	But I want something . . . well, sophisticated.
Photographer	Sophisticated?
Director	Yeah. What else is there in the story?
Lavinia	A stable.
Director	Out of the question. This is Ealing, not Hollywood.
Lavinia	Shepherds then.
Director	Yes, of course. Can you sort it out?
Lavinia	No problem.
	(*She goes and gets some costumes. These are not necessarily all that appropriate, which will add to the amusement. Her 'extras' can be members of the congregation.*)
Lavinia	Right. We need shepherds. (*She persuades people to come on stage.*)
Director	From Jaws 6 . . . to this! What a come down! Hurry up, you lot! This is a Christmas card, not an Easter card.
Photographer	Yes . . . either side of Mary and Joseph. Close in a bit. (*Places shepherds with a few more encouraging words.*) That's fine. Now . . . a big smile for Christmas!
Director	No. Hang on. We need some . . . pizzazz! Hey, I've got it. There were these three wise men in the story. Bit of class.

	Lavinia . . . three wise men please.
Lavinia	Three wise men. Dunno about wise, but I'll do my best with the three men. (*She brings them on.*)
Photographer	I thought they were kings in the story?
Director	Kings, wise men . . . who cares? I'm not even sure about the men.
Photographer	Yes. (*More stage directions to the subjects*) Hold the pressies where we can see them. Fine. Hold it . . . come in a bit please. Big smile for Christmas!
Director	Nearly . . . but it needs to be, well, a bit more special. What's the word? Holy, yes that's it. We need to make it a bit more holy. Yes. We must have angels. Lavinia?
Lavinia	Sorry, we're right out of haloes!
Director	Dressing room budget a bit tight, is it?
Photographer	Great! You look fine as you are! Hold it . . . big smile for Christmas.
Director	(*Moves in front of the camera*) Carol singers! That's it, carol singers! Lavinia, grab 'em.
Photographer	Where on earth am I going to put them?
Director	In a small semi-circle, over there.
Photographer	(*Stage directions for carol singers*) Come on . . . as if you are under a lamp-post. Closer together – it's supposed to be cold.
Director	We haven't even got a lamp-post.
Photographer	(*Further directions*) Big smile for Christmas!
	(*He is interrupted by the arrival of a couple of yuppies.*)
Nigel	Is this the party? We've got the bubbly.
Director	To what do I owe this interruption?
Letitia	Christmas. It's all about partying. Isn't it, Nigel?
Nigel	You got it, Letty. We're the life and soul of a party.
Director	Get out of here. (*Short pause*) No, wait! *That's* the modern touch. Lavinia!
Photographer	OK, Harry, can you stand here please?
Nigel	It's Nigel actually.

Photographer	OK, Caroline. Just there.
Letitia	Letitia!
Photographer	Bless you dear! (*Moves Nigel and Letitia into position*) Ready now . . . big smile for Christmas!
Director	Christmas! Of course. We've missed the main man. Lavinia! You've got to get him for me.
Lavinia	Main man? You don't mean . . .you don't mean the vicar, do you?
Director	You're right. I don't mean the vicar.
Lavinia	Oh!
Director	It's obvious. We need Father Christmas.
Lavinia	Of course. (*She brings on Father Christmas, who stands at the front and gets in the way of Mary and Joseph.*)
Photographer	Right in the centre please. Lavinia? Thank you. Now . . . a big smile for Christmas. (*Baby cries.*)
Director	That's all I need! Lavinia! Get that child out of here. (*Turns to photographer*) Now – shoot!
Photographer	(*Pause as photographer prepares himself for the picture and for his big last line*) ALL OF YOU . . . A BIG SMILE FOR CHRISTMAS! (*Flash goes off.*)
Director	Now, that's what I call Christmas!
	(*Pause, all exit.*)

Peter Comaish

Gifts

A Christmas gift service

Bible references
Matthew 1.18 – 2.12
2 Corinthians 8.1-9

Processional hymn   'Lord Jesus Christ' (HON 311)

Welcome

Introduction to theme   *Ask people why we give gifts at Christmas, then write up the suggestions on an overhead projector or a flip chart and explore them with the congregation.*

Then rehearse a Christmas shout:

'Jesus is born,

Jesus is born,

Jesus is born for us!'

Poem   (*It works well if the person reciting the poem knows it by heart, and Christmas carols are played quietly in the background.*)

> Aunty likes smellies, and uncle needs wellies,
> And granny loves china to put on display.
> For grandad some slippers, our cat two fat kippers,
> But what shall we give to the child in the hay?
>
> For dear cousin Rosy, a patterned tea cosy,
> And two-year-old Daniel wants a trumpet to play.
> A drum for his brother, and ear muffs for Mother,
> But what shall we give to the child in the hay?
>
> For our sister Susie, a mini jacuzzi,
> And a bike for our Peter would just make his day.
> And Roger supposes his girlfriend loves roses,
> But what shall we give to the child in the hay?

For Dad some old brandy would come in very handy,
And for our mum a surprise holiday.
So our list is now ended, our money expended,
And nothing is left for the child in the hay.

Presentation of gifts   *In our church we ask children from the Sunday groups and uni-formed organizations to bring small wrapped gifts to the service. This is in response to the annual appeal by our local mental hospital trust for presents for patients and residents of group homes. They supply a list of possible items. Each present is marked as suitable for a man or lady, and the Brownies decorate two large boxes to receive the gifts when they are brought up during the service. A representative of the trust talks about its work and speaks about what Christmas is like in its homes.*

Hymn   'In the bleak mid-winter' (HON 248) (*Sing this while the gifts are presented.*)

Prayer time   A present list for Jesus. *Distribute pencils and paper to the congrega-tion. Explain that instead of writing a present list for ourselves and sending it to Santa, we are going to write or draw a list of presents we should like people in need at Christmas to be given by Jesus. Suggest categories, such as friendship for the lonely, comfort for the sad, food for the hungry, shelter for the homeless, healing for the sick, and so on. Play the last verse of the previous carol while everyone is doing this. Then invite them to come up and fix their prayer with blutak or a pin onto a display board. When they have all done so, end with a short period of silence, followed by a prayer for the recipients of your gifts, and the Lord's Prayer.*

Offertory hymn   'The Virgin Mary had a baby boy' (HON 496)

Reading   2 Corinthians 8.1-9

Christmas unlocked

This involves a bit of advance preparation, but the congregation will particularly enjoy being involved in the search for the case.

You will need:

1.   A large package, gift-wrapped, full of packaging materials and nothing else save the message 'EXmas, Christmas without Jesus'. Ensure the package has some weight so that it feels like a real present.

2.   A rather smaller brown paper parcel containing a key with the label 'This will unlock the real meaning of Christmas'.

3.   A locked case containing a candle, a bread roll, a map, a Bible, and a model or picture of a manger with baby Jesus in it.

4.   Five placards with the words:

I am the light of the world
I am the bread of life
I am the way
I am the truth
I am the life.

Before the service, hide the case containing the five objects in church.

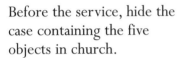

Talk   Introduce the subject of guessing what we are going to get for Christmas.

Produce the first parcel. Invite suggestions as to what it contains. Ask for some children to come and feel it. Get one to unwrap it. Ask for reactions. Sometimes we are disappointed by Christmas. It seems to promise so much but delivers so little.

Produce the second parcel. Adopt a similar routine. When the key is found, institute a search for something to unlock. Have the case opened and display the contents. Get the congregation to try to guess what they have to do about unlocking the meaning of Christmas. Reinforce the correct guesses by displaying the placards.

Suggest to them to try and include one or two of these objects among their Christmas decorations to remind them of the meaning of the festival.

Action song   'Little Jesus, sweetly sleep' (HON 306)

Distribution of gifts   *Remind everyone that Christmas is about both giving and receiving, then give all the children a small gift, such as a Christmas tree decoration or some sweets.*

Final prayer and blessing

Christmas shout

Hymn   'Joy to the world' (HON 283)

Donald Dowling

Christmas pop-up card

Try this idea for a lively and unusual Christmas card.

You will need:

Two pieces of A4 card

Scissors

Four paper fasteners

Felt-tips and crayons

Fold one of the pieces of card in half. On the front of the Christmas card, draw a picture of the stable door and a star.

On the second sheet of card, draw and cut out two figures to represent one of the kings and Mary and the baby. Cut out a strip of card to be used as a lever on the pop-up card.

Cut a slit in the front of the card.

Attach the figures of the king and Mary to the card with the top fasteners. Use the bottom fasteners to attach the figures to the lever inside the card. Write 'Happy Christmas' inside the card and add your own decorative designs.

Jon Webster

slit

Paper fasteners

Write a greeting at the base of the card

Top fasteners join the figures to the card

Lever

HAPPY CHRISTMAS

Bottom fasteners join the figures to the lever

Try to get as much space as you can between the top and bottom fasteners

Teachings of Jesus

The sower

A sketch children will enjoy performing, with a straightforward interpretation of the parable of the sower.

Bible references
Matthew 13.1-23

Mark 4.1-20

Luke 8.1-15

Cast
Farmer, four Hearers, Narrator, Friend, two Enquirers, Reader

Props
Large Bible

(While the first part is being read, the Farmer comes and sows seed from the back.)

Narrator   One day Jesus began to teach by the lake. He taught many things by parables, and in his teaching said:

Once there was a man who went out to sow corn. As he scattered the seed in the field, some of it fell along the path, and the birds came and ate it up. Some of it fell on rocky ground, where there was little soil. The seeds soon sprouted, because the soil wasn't deep. But when the sun came up, it burned the young plants; and because the roots had not grown deep enough, the plants soon dried up. Some of the seed fell among thorn bushes, which grew up and choked the plants. But some seeds fell in good soil, and the plants produced corn; some produced a hundred grains, others sixty, and others thirty (Matthew 13.3–8).

(Hearers enter and sit in a semi-circle at the front. Enquirers enter and stand to one side. The Reader stands at the back holding a large Bible, reading.)

Enquirer 1   I wonder why Jesus told that story.

Enquirer 2   Yes, it was a good way to show how people sowed their corn in those times, but I can't see that it is much help to us nowadays.

Enquirer 1   Maybe there's a hidden meaning behind the story.

Enquirer 2   I wonder what it might be.

(They exit.)

Narrator   This is what the parable means. Those who hear the message about the kingdom but do not understand it are like the seeds that fell along the path. The evil one comes and snatches away what was sown in them.

(*Hearer 1 comes to the front.*)

Hearer 1   All this talk about God. I don't understand it. I'm off. (*Exit.*)

Narrator   The seeds that fell on rocky ground stand for those who receive the message gladly as soon as they hear it. But it does not sink deep into them and they do not last long. So, when trouble or persecution comes because of the message, they give up at once.

Hearer 2   (*Gets up and comes to the front*) I like all this about God's love. I'm going to be a Christian.

(*Hearer 1 enters with a Friend. They see Hearer 2 and stop. Hearer 1 points a finger at Hearer 2.*)

Hearer 1   Look at her, she's a Christian!

Friend   She isn't really, is she? She must be stupid.

Hearer 1   Yes, that's right. Completely stupid.

(*They laugh and go off stage chanting, 'She is stupid, completely stupid.'*)

Hearer 2   Oh dear! They used to be my friends. I don't like being laughed at like that. Maybe being a Christian isn't really a very good idea. Perhaps I'd better forget about it all. (*Starts to go after the others.*)

(*Shouts*) Hey, wait for me! You're wrong. I'm not a Christian any more. (*Runs off after the others.*)

Narrator   The seeds that fell among thorn bushes stand for those who hear the message, but the worries of this life and the love of riches choke the message and they don't bear fruit.

(*Hearer 3 comes up and stands centre front.*)

Hearer 3   I am definitely going to be a Christian. I think this idea of Jesus dying for me so that my sins can be forgiven is very important. Well, I do plenty of things that I shouldn't and I could do with being forgiven. I'd like to make a new, clean start.

(*Hearers 1 and 2 and Friend enter again.*)

Hearer 1   Hi there! We always go down town on a Sunday morning. Coming with us?

Hearer 3   Well, no. Not on a Sunday morning.

Hearer 1   Please yourself. (*They exit.*)

Hearer 3 (*Pauses*) You'll never guess what we were told at school today. From now on, we're going to have twice as much homework at the weekends. *And* a maths test every Monday. *A maths test!* I'll have to revise for that every weekend too. How am I going to fit it all in, and still have some time to enjoy myself? (*Sighs*) Oh well, I could always do a couple of hours' work on a Sunday morning and then go down and join the others in town. Pity about church.

Narrator And the seeds sown in the good soil stand for those who hear the message and understand it. They bear fruit, some as much as a hundred, others sixty, and others thirty.

(*Hearer 4 comes to centre front.*)

Hearer 4 I am going to let Jesus into my life. I want to please him and follow his plan, come what may. I know that he will always be with me and look after me wherever I go.

(*Hearer 4 exits. The Reader comes forward and stands centre stage.*)

Narrator (*Reading from the Bible*) No eye has seen, no ear has heard, no mind has conceived what God has prepared for those who love him (1 Corinthians 2.9).

Barbara Rohde

The great party

Bible references

Matthew 22.1-14

Luke 14.16-24

Cast

Master, Servant, three Friends, Crowd

Props

Invitations

Master	I am going to have a big party and will invite all my friends. We'll have a great time. We'll have pizzas, beefburgers, hot dogs, ice-cream and chocolate sauce, jelly and a huge chocolate cake. Afterwards we'll have a disco with a live band, the best I can hire. Servant, come here please. Take these invitations and deliver them to my friends.
Servant	Yes sir. (*He goes to each Friend in turn.*)
	(*To first Friend*) My master would like to invite you to his party.
1st Friend	Thank you very much. It sounds great.
Servant	(*To second Friend*) Here is an invitation to my master's party.
2nd Friend	Thank you very much. I'd love to come.
Servant	(*To third Friend*) My master asked me to give you this invitation.
3rd Friend	Oh, a party. Of course I'll come.
	(*Servant returns home.*)
Master	Servant. My party is now ready. Would you please go and tell all my friends that it is time to come.
Servant	Yes sir. (*Servant goes to each Friend in turn.*)
	(*To first Friend*) Everything is ready for the party. Please come now.
1st Friend	Oh, I have bought a new computer and it's just been delivered. I must stay and unpack it and make sure that it is all right. I'm so sorry.
Servant	(*To second Friend*) The party is ready. Please will you come now.
2nd Friend	Oh, I'm so sorry. I've just got a new mountain bike and I simply must try it out. I'm sorry that I won't be able to come.
Servant	(*To third Friend*) Please come now. The party is ready.
3rd Friend	I've just got a new boyfriend and he's invited me out this evening. I'm so sorry. I won't be able to come after all.
	(*Servant returns to Master.*)
Servant	I'm so sorry, sir. None of them can come. One has got to unpack a computer that's just been delivered. Another has got to try out a new mountain bike, and another is being taken out by a new boyfriend. They all say they are very sorry.
Master	(*Angrily*) Excuses, excuses, that's all it is! Hurry out into the streets and alleys of the town, and bring back anyone you can find.

(*Servant goes out into the town and brings them all in.*)

Servant   You are all invited to my master's marvellous party.

(*Servant goes to Master.*)

I have done what you said, sir, and still there is room for more.

Master   Go out into the country roads and lanes and make people come in, so that my house will be full. I tell you all that no one who was invited will taste the food at my party.

Barbara Rohde

Party rap

This rap requires plenty of movement, plenty of excitement and some simple strong movements to go with the words. To get the rhythm right, we used a backing tape, recorded using a drum machine. The choruses can be shouted out by a group of people, building up to a dramatic finish on the last one. The verses are probably best delivered by one or two mobile rappers, dancing around at the front of the stage, with the chorus of voices behind them.

Bible references

Matthew 22.1-14

Luke 14.16-24

Heard about the party? There's raving tonight!
It's gonna be crazy, gonna be all right.
Everyone's welcome who'll give me some skin:
bring your body for dancing, bring your friends poppin'.

      Well that's OK, now don't be left out,
      this is where it's at, there ain't no doubt.

The first one said, 'No way José,
gotta earn my bread, can't party today.'
The second one said, 'Look I bought a Mercedes,
gotta follow the lights and go chasing the ladies.'

      Well that's too bad, you'll be left out,
      this is where it's at, there ain't no doubt.

The third one said, 'Man I just got wed,
so why should I leave my marriage bed?'
'No guys! What's your game?
If they won't come running, bring the blind and the lame.'

      Whoever you are, don't be left out,
      this is where it's at, there ain't no doubt.

And the boss said, 'Yeah! There'll still be room!
Bring everyone along who's tired of the gloom.'
The tramp said, 'Sure, that'll be cool,
but ain't this guy a crazy old fool?'

      Well, not at all, only fools are left out,
      if you want to go heaven, gotta move, gotta shout!

Peter Comaish

Water of life

Bible references

John 4.1-26

Psalm 65

Invitation to worship

Leader   We have come together today to worship God, who created the universe, sending life-giving water to the earth, and who, by his grace, gives us new life in Christ, filling us with the Holy Spirit.

Jesus said, 'Whoever drinks the water that I will give them will never be thirsty again.'

Come, let us sing for joy to the Lord;

All   **let us shout aloud to the Rock of our salvation**.

Leader   The sea is his, for he made it,

All   **and his hands formed the dry land**.

Leader   Come, let us bow down in worship,

All   **Let us kneel before the Lord our Maker**. (*From Psalm 95.*)

Hymn   'Fill your hearts with joy and gladness' (HTC 30)

Prayer   (*This can be read by one or more adults, with children saying the response.*)

We thank you Lord and give you praise.

In the beginning the Holy Spirit moved over the surface of the waters
and life was created.

We thank you Lord and give you praise.

By the gift of water all life is nourished and sustained.

We thank you Lord and give you praise.

Through the waters of the Red Sea you led your people out of slavery
to freedom in the promised land.

We thank you Lord and give you praise.

In the waters of Jordan your Son was baptized by John and anointed
with the Holy Spirit.

We thank you Lord and give you praise.

By the death and resurrection of your Son, you have freed us from
bondage to sin and death and opened to us eternal life.

We thank you Lord and give you praise.

By the water of life flowing from the throne of the Lamb, you bring
healing to the nations.

We thank you Lord and give you praise.

Confession

Leader   Through Christ our sins are washed away. Let us confess our sins to
God.

All   **Almighty and merciful God**
               we have sinned against you
               in thought, word and deed.
               We have not loved you with all our heart.
               We have not loved others as Christ loves us.
               We are truly sorry.

> **In your mercy, forgive what we have been,**
> **Help us to amend what we are,**
> **and direct what we shall be;**
> **that we may delight in your will**
> **and walk in your ways,**
> **to the glory and praise of your name. Amen.**

Leader God our Father, who by our Lord Jesus Christ has reconciled the world to himself and forgives the sins of all who truly repent, pardon and deliver us from all our sins, and grant us the grace and power of the Holy Spirit. **Amen.**

Song 'Peace is flowing like a river' (SHF 431)

Psalm (*From Psalm 65. Divide the congregation into two groups to do this.*)

Leader Oh God, it is right to praise you, because you answer our prayers:

You care for the land and water it,

A **and make it rich and fertile.**

Leader You fill the running streams with water,

B **and irrigate the land.**

Leader You soften the ground with showers,

A **and make the young crops grow.**

Leader You crown the year with goodness,

B **and give us a plentiful harvest.**

Leader The fields are covered with grain,

All **they shout with joy and sing. Amen.**

Reading Genesis 7.1-10

Hymn 'Come let us join our cheerful songs' (HTC 206)

Reading John 4.7-14

Talk   Water means many things to us. Here are some things that I have brought along that are all connected with water. Can you guess why they are important? (*Have the necessary props ready to give to children to hold at the front as each is mentioned.*)

Watering can   Plants need water to live and grow.

Glass of water   We also need water to live and grow. Without it, we can live only a few days.

Life jacket   Water can sometimes be dangerous. We could need one of these to keep us afloat if we got into trouble.

Model ark   Noah needed a boat to carry him, his family and a whole load of animals to safety. It was their home for 150 very crowded days.

Sponge   Not everyone likes the idea, but we need water for washing.

Beach ball   Sometimes it's good just to splash around and have fun in the water.

All of these symbols to do with water have meaning for us as Christians too. Let's see what they remind us of.

* The *watering can* and *glass of water* remind us that we need God to live and grow.

* The *life jacket* keeps people safe. We can turn to God at any time to ask for protection.

* Just as Noah's *ark* must have been a squash, with not all the people and animals necessarily getting on all the time, so we are together as the family of the Church.

* We are all on the same journey together. Is this why the boat is an ancient symbol for the Church? It is currently used by the World Council of Churches.

* The *sponge* for washing reminds us that by the death and resurrection of Jesus we are washed clean from sin.

* Finally, let's not forget that sometimes we can just *splash about* in the Holy Spirit and enjoy the joy of the Lord.

These things are all ours as we let the Holy Spirit work in us. Remember the promise of Jesus: 'Let anyone who is thirsty come to me.'

Baptismal creed

Leader   Do you believe and trust in God the Father who made you and all life?

All   **I believe and trust in him.**

Leader   Do you believe and trust in his Son Jesus Christ who redeemed you and all humankind?

All   **I believe and trust in him.**

Leader   Do you believe and trust in his Holy Spirit who gives life to you and all the people of God?

All   **I believe and trust in him.**

Leader   This is the faith of the Church.

All   **This is our faith. We believe and trust in one God, Father, Son and Holy Spirit.**

Hymn   'Water of life, cleanse and refresh us' (CHFE 401)

Prayer

EITHER

In peace we pray to you, Lord God.

For all people in their daily life and work,
remembering especially seafarers, fishermen and all
who depend on the sea for their living,
for our families, friends and neighbours
and for those who are alone.

For this community, our nation and for the world,
for all who work for justice, freedom and peace.

For the right use of your creation, especially
of your precious gift of water,
for the victims of hunger, drought, fear,
injustice or oppression.

For all in danger, sorrow or any kind of trouble,
for those who serve all who are sick, friendless
or in need.

For the peace, mission and unity of the Church,
for all who proclaim the gospel
and for all who search for truth.

For our own special needs and concerns today.

OR

Place a vase filled with water centrally. Scatter flowers on the table or floor around the vase. Explain that the flowers need to be put back in contact with the water in order to live. We need to be in contact with God to be whole and to know life in all its fullness.

Ask the congregation to pray, in silence, for people and situations they know that need the life-giving Spirit given by Jesus. Invite them to place one of the scattered flowers back in the vase as a token of their prayer in silence or, if appropriate, with a brief explanation of their prayer. When the vase is full it is placed either on the altar or at the front of the church.

The Lord's Prayer

Hymn   'O, the deep, deep love of Jesus' (HTC 465)

The blessing

Lord God, the well-spring of life,

pour into our hearts the living water of your grace:

increase our faith,

and grant that we may serve you

in your life-giving strength,

through Jesus Christ our Lord. **Amen.**

Go in peace and serve the Lord.

Thanks be to God.

Adrian Legg

Christ, the light of the world

Bible references

John 1.1-18

John 8.12

The theme of Christ's light entering our world of darkness is a particularly evocative one, but perhaps even more so when we meet together to worship during the dark months of winter. The service focuses on how Christ reveals God to us and is a guide for each of us in knowing and following him.

Preparation

- *Candle — one for each member of the congregation to take home at the end of the service.*

- *Candle holders. Cut out card circles (about 15 cm in diameter) with a hole just large enough to insert a candle.*

- *Bike light, electric bulb, lamp, lantern and other kinds of lights.*

Choose some members of the congregation in advance to help with the procession and the lighting of candles later in the service.

Hand out the card circles and candles to the congregation as they arrive for the service.

Processional song   *Congregation sing 'Within our darkest night' (HON 562) while the choir or group process to the front with lighted candles and light the main candles on the altar.*

Introductory sentence   Jesus said, 'I am the light of the world. Whoever follows me will never walk in darkness, but will have the light of life' (John 8.12).

Offertory hymn   'Christ is the world's true light' (HON 78)

Confession

Use the following response after each confession:

Jesus, light of the world,
shine in our darkness.

Lord Jesus Christ, we confess our sins before you.

Forgive us, we pray, for the times we shun your light
and prefer to hide in the darkness of our hearts . . .

Forgive us, we pray, for the times we do not stand up for your
truth but hide in the darkness . . .

Forgive us, we pray, for our own selfishness and greed . . .

Forgive us, we pray, for the harmful things we do and say
to others . . .

Forgive us, we pray,

that we live by the light of our own eyes

and not by your light of truth . . .

Collect for the second Sunday after Christmas

Gloria *Use a traditional setting or a lively modern version such as the Peruvian gloria 'Glory to God' (HON 161).*

Reading Jeremiah 31.7-14

Introduction to the Gospel reading: How can we see God? *Blindfold a 'volunteer' from the congregation and ask them to identify various objects such as an orange or hairbrush by feeling them. Then give them a drawing and see if they can tell you what it is.*

The last task was impossible to do. How could the blindfolded person be expected to see the drawing?

In the same way, many people feel it is impossible to know God, because we cannot see him. How can we know what he is like if we cannot see him? This Gospel reading tells us that God has given us a special way by which we can see him. Can you work out what it is from the reading?

Reading John 1.1-18 *As this is a long reading, you might wish to use just verses 1–9, or to choose a group in advance to read the version in* The Dramatised Bible.

Hymn 'The light of Christ' (MP 223)

Talk We use many different kinds of light to help us to see during dark evenings. Which do you use?

Show your assortment of lights – light bulb, bike light, candle, lantern, and so on. Discuss how these are used and for what purpose.

Each of these lights has a special purpose. We have been looking at a different kind of light today – the light of Christ. What is special about the light of Christ?

It is a REVEALING light.

The Gospel reading tells us that Christ reveals God to us. Because he is God's own Son, he can show us what God is like.

It is a SAVING light.

Just as a lighthouse saves ships from being shipwrecked on rocks hidden in the darkness, so Christ saves us from all that is wrong and brings us back to God.

It is a GUIDING light.

Just as a bike light or lantern shows us the right path forward, so Christ is our guide throughout life to show us the way we should live.

The creed

Song   'Lord the light of your love' (HON 317)

Congregational activity

Prayer candles

On the card circle, the congregation should write or draw pictures of people, nations or events that they want to pray for. You might want to give some suggestions of things to pray for, such as recent national and local events, their families and the sick. Ask them to write a prayer or draw a picture of something they want to ask God about for themselves and then insert the candle in the holder. Suggest that these prayer candles might be used regularly during the coming year as they pray for these people.

Prayers/intercessions   *When people have finished drawing and writing on their candle holders, have the group that processed in at the beginning of the service come to the front and light their candles from the altar. They light the candles of the people seated at the ends of the pews, who then light the candles of the people sitting next to them. Ensure that there are enough adults strategically placed to supervise the younger children during this activity.*

Sing traditional Christmas carols, or songs such as 'Colours of Day' (HON 87) and 'The Lord is my light' (HON 486) during the lighting of the candles.

Allow a time of silence as the congregation prays for the people and events on their candles.

Finish by saying The Lord's Prayer together.

The blessing

Leader   God sends us out in the light of Christ

to bring light into our world of darkness.

May the light of Christ so shine in our hearts

that we might bring his light to others.

And the blessing of God almighty,

the Father, the Son, and the Holy Spirit,

be among you and remain with you always.

Amen.

Recessional song   'We are marching in the light of God' (*Jump Up if you're Wearing Red*, p.34)

During this song, the congregation should process to the back of the church, with candles still lit.

James Bryce

Nobody's perfect

In this play, based on the parable of the Good Samaritan, each person sees in the others what he wants to see. Only the Samaritan sees in the wounded man a fellow child of God — the whole person.

Bible reference

Luke 10. 25-37

Cast

Two Travellers, Robbers, Priest, Levite, Samaritan

The scene is set on the desert road to Jericho.

(Enter two Travellers.)

Traveller 1 Well, this is where I turn off.

Traveller 2 Oh, I thought you were going all the way to Jericho?

Traveller 1 No, 'fraid not. Well, it's been interesting hearing about your shops and the fleet of ships and your contract with the army.

Traveller 2 And did I mention the timber business? You must have my card. Here we are. (*Hands card to Traveller 1.*) Any cedar of Lebanon you want at *very* special prices!

Traveller 1 Most kind. (*Whistles to off-stage Robbers.*) Glad to have met you. (*Hits Traveller 2 on the head.*)

    (*Robbers appear and proceed to mug and rob Traveller 2.*)

Traveller 2 But I don't understand. Why are you doing this?

Traveller 1 You've bored me with your business, now I'm boring you with mine. Tie him up! (*Robbers do so.*) Right, let's go.

Traveller 2 You can't leave me here! I'll die. You've taken all my money and my letters of credit.

Traveller 1 (*Returning*) Letters of credit, eh? For Jericho? Thanks very much. Well, off we go.

Traveller 2 You can't leave me like this!

Traveller 1   Perhaps you're right. (*Hits him again.*) OK, men, Jericho it is.

              (*Traveller 1 and robbers exit. Traveller 2 groans and struggles feebly. Enter priest.*)

Traveller 2   Help me!

Priest   (*Stops.*) Help you? No thanks! We've been warned about you hitch-hikers. It's a scam. You'll attack me for sure.

Traveller 2   I won't. You're a priest! Help me!

Priest   I am indeed a priest. If you know that, you also know that I must not be made unclean. Look at you. You're a disgrace and disgusting.

Traveller 2   Please!

Priest   I am on official Temple business. Do you realize that you are obstructing the work of God?

Traveller 2	Look at me! I am Joshua ben Isaak. I am a regular contributor to the Temple funds. You must know me.
Priest	I see only a dirty obstruction. I cannot wait. God's business calls.
	(*Exit Priest. Enter Levite.*)
Traveller 2	Sir, sir, please help me! Robbers have attacked me and taken all I possess.
Levite	Attacked you?
Traveller 2	Yes.
Levite	Have you nothing?
Traveller 2	All is gone! I lie here in the middle of the desert begging your help.
Levite	There must be a reason for this.
Traveller 2	A reason?
Levite	God must be punishing you. What have you done, you wretched man?
Traveller 2	I have done nothing. I am a God-fearing man. You are a Levite?
Levite	Yes, and I know that the Law of God is undefiled and searches the soul. You are a sinner, obviously.
Traveller 2	(*Wailing*) I'm not, I'm not! At least no more than anyone else.
Levite	Lies will not help you. Phwah! (*Waves in disgust.*) Let the father of lies have you.
	(*Exit Levite. Enter Samaritan.*)
Traveller 2	Help me!
Samaritan	(*Stops*) Yes? Oh, you poor man.
Traveller 2	Stop! You are a Samaritan. You cannot help me.
Samaritan	Cannot?
Traveller 2	(*Sinks down*) Will not.
Samaritan	I can and I will! Are we not both God's children and each of great value to him?
	(*Freeze.*)

Anthony Geering

Events of Jesus' life

The wedding party

This sketch was written to arouse children's curiosity so that they will look at the Bible to check out the stories for themselves. Obviously for younger children, either watching or joining in this play will introduce them to one of the events of Jesus' ministry. But for older children it opens the way for deeper exploration of the rich layers of symbolism and meaning in the Gospel account of Jesus' first miracle. It is an example of the extravagant generosity of God who in Jesus gives us 'life in all its fullness'. The abundant provision of new wine marks both an ending and a beginning – the old wine of Judaism being replaced by the new wine of the kingdom, and the beginning of a new era looking forward to the wedding banquet in heaven. When we break bread and share wine in the sacrament, it is a foretaste of that heavenly banquet. By comparison with that celebration, with the new wine of the kingdom, all worldly festivity is flat and dull and leaves a nasty taste in the mouth.

The sketch was written as a radio play. It can be read by members of a children's group to all the others, or presented to a wider audience as a play. Stage direction is minimal to allow for creative adaptation as circumstances permit.

Bible reference

John 2.1-11

Cast

Two Servants and Voice

Props

Wine jars or bottles

Servant 1   What a party! I'm run off my feet. When do you think it will end?

Servant 2   Soon, I hope. I'm tired too. This party has gone on for too long as far as I'm concerned.

Voice   Bring some more wine!

Servant 1   (*Gets up, moves across to wine casks.*) Hey, this wine is getting a bit low. I do hope that the party ends soon. There is only enough left for this serving by the looks of things.

Servant 2   Hang on. Before you get too worried, I'll go down to the cellar to see if there's any more.

(*Both go about their duties, then meet again.*)

Servant 1   Any luck with more wine?

Servant 2   No more left down there. I don't remember bringing up the last barrel. Must have been some time ago and I've forgotten already. Gosh I am tired. How much is left in that barrel?

Servant 1   Not a lot. Think of the disgrace if the wine runs out now. All those guests.

Servant 2   I know. It wouldn't be so bad if the boss wasn't in the trade. We have the finest vineyard for miles around. I feel sure that most of the guests only came to try the wine.

Servant 1   Yes, and it looks as if it's just about to run out at his son's wedding feast. What shall we do?

Servant 2   I'll go and see if I can have a quiet word with the boss. Perhaps he can send out for some more, borrow from the neighbours like.

Servant 1   Don't be daft! He won't want to take in someone else's wine. You know how he's always boasting about the quality of his own. Mind you, I don't know what he is going to do. Owning fine vineyards is one thing, but when there is no wine to drink – well, you may just as well own a weed bed.

Servant 2   (*Goes out and then returns looking sad.*) The boss has taken it very bad. He doesn't know what to do. I did suggest that he borrows from a neighbour, but the only one whose wine is any good is old Eli – and he's one of the guests.

Voice   Bring some more wine!

Servant 1   Well, that's it. That's the end of that. They've drunk us dry. I'll take this last jug in and tell the boss that the party is over.

(*Goes out, then returns looking surprised.*) Guess what? Someone out there said don't worry. Just serve water from now on.

Servant 2   Water! It's more than my job's worth. I enjoy working here. Are you sure? I'll go and double check.

Servant 1   OK. You check. Perhaps I didn't hear right. What with the worry and being tired . . . but the man who said it sounded so sure. I didn't know what to say. I just hurried out here.

Servant 2   You must be crazy. Can you imagine the scandal? The owner of the best vineyard in the district serving water at his son's wedding. It will finish him. He'll never be able to sell another bottle.

Servant 1   You're right – nobody wants to pay for wine and get a bottle of water. People will always be suspicious with that sort of reputation. Yes, you go and check with the man who talked to me. He didn't seem to be the type to make a laughing-stock of the master. You'll find him easily. He's with a whole bunch of friends.

Servant 2   (*Goes out and then returns.*)

(*Briskly*) OK. Fill the water jars – all of them. Then take the guests a drink. Go on! Be brave. I'll be right behind you.

Servant 1   Yes, right behind me. But don't get too close. I want room to run off. I don't like it. It sounds bad to me. I think we should do this together, then we can share the blame. The boss is unlikely to fire both of us. Who would be left to do the work?

(They both go through the process of filling the water jars, then drawing it out into serving jugs and taking it out into the guest area.)

(Back in the kitchen.)

Servant 2   I can't understand it. They like it. They are all saying it tastes better than the wine we were serving earlier.

Servant 1   I know, I know. Look at them – all gathered around the boss, singing his praises, and wondering at such fine wine from his vineyards.

Servant 2   I can't understand this. I am going to break the rules and taste this drink.

Servant 1   Go ahead. There is no rule against us drinking water while we are serving the guests.

Servant 2   That's true. After all, you and I know that it's water in these jars. *(He takes a sip.)* Gosh! Our water . . . that water we poured into these jars . . . it's the most glorious wine. It's beautiful – even better than the best wine we have ever produced!

Servant 1   I don't understand this. You and I filled those jars with water . . . didn't we?

Servant 2   We did. But you go ahead and taste it now!

Robert Cuin

The man born blind
An all-age service

Bible reference

John 9.1-8

Preparation

1. General

Find out about a blind charity such as:

- Royal National Institute for the Blind
- Sight Savers
- Guide Dogs for the Blind
- Talking Newspapers for the Blind.

If you have a blind person in your congregation you might consider asking whether he/she would be willing to be interviewed. An alternative might be to interview someone involved with a charity for the blind, someone working in a hospital eye department, an optician, or a teacher of the blind. Obviously you need to work out your interview in advance.

2. Games

Either

(a) a blindfold Kim's game

You will need: two blindfolds and ten articles which have a distinctive shape, texture or smell. Possibilities might include an orange, a pear, an egg cup, a tennis ball, a bar of perfumed soap, a bath sponge, a small cuddly toy, a comb, a tube of tooth-paste (ensure cap is secure!), a bunch of keys. Place on a tray and cover with a cloth.

To play

The blindfolded contestants have two minutes in which to feel the objects. Cover them up again and get them to whisper to an assistant the objects they remember. Share the results with the congregation. Ask contestants whether they found it hard or easy.

Or

(b) A blindfold taste game

You will need:

Five small dishes containing

(i)   Spaghetti/baked beans

(ii)   Chocolate mousse or yoghurt

(iii)   Mint toothpaste

(iv)   Flavoured jelly

(v)   Marmite/paste sandwich.

Two blindfolds, spoons, a towel and a couple of glasses of water to take away the taste. A covering cloth.

To play

Blindfold each contestant and get each in turn to taste from the dishes, asking them to guess what they have eaten. Alternate between them. At the end remove blind-folds and help them clean up! Ask each to say how they made their guesses, e.g. taste, texture, smell, etc. Would they normally choose to eat blindfolded, and if not why?

3.   You might also find a **Braille book** and/or **tape for the blind** useful.

Order of service

Begin with a hymn of praise, such as:

'O for a thousand tongues to sing' (HON 362)

'Christ, whose glory fills the skies' (HON 82)

Welcome by the leader   Today we are basing our service around the story of the healing by Jesus of the man born blind. If you are blind you have to rely on your other senses to help you. *Ask for the names of the other senses. Write down the answers on a flip chart or OHP if available.*

They should mention:

Hearing

Touch

Taste

Smell.

Now we are going to have a game that involves using one or more of the other senses. *Invite a couple of victims or volunteers.*

Play either Kim's game or the taste game above.

Action song   'Two little eyes' (JP 262)

Prayer of thanksgiving for our senses

The following prayer could be used:

Thank you, Father, for eyes that can see the patterns of light in a sunlit world, the colours of a rainbow, the shape of a smile on a friend's face.

Thank you, Father, for being able to feel a hug from a friend, the warmth of a fire, the soft fur of a pet.

Thank you, Father, for being able to smell the aroma of newly baked bread or the fragrance of a flower.

Thank you, Father, for being able to taste the sharp, crisp flavour of an apple, or the smooth dark savour of chocolate.

Help us not to take our senses for granted, for they are your gifts. **Amen.**

Reading   John 9.1-8. The healing of the blind man.

Hymn   'Amazing grace' (HON 27)

Leader   The story we have just heard shows how Jesus healed a man born blind. It was a miracle. Today some forms of blindness can be cured by a simple but delicate operation. In some countries medical teams run eye camps which bring sight to hundreds of sufferers from blindness. Some eye conditions, however, cannot be easily cured, so there are several charities which support blind people and the partially sighted. Blind people can also learn to read with Braille books (*produce one if available*), or they can hear books or newspapers read on tape.

We are now going to meet X who is blind/works with a blind charity.

Interview   *(This should be worked out in advance.) Draw out the positive things that can be done or achieved by blind people. If interviewing a representative of a blind charity, ask them about their society, their particular work and, if appropriate, how sighted people can support it.*

Offertory hymn   'Father, I place into your hands' (HON 121)

Prayer time   *(Arrange for four children to come forward with an unlit candle. Prime four other members of the congregation to come up with a short bidding on a card.)*

Topics might include:

1.   *Those who are blind or partially sighted.*

2.   *Those who give medical or ophthalmic help to the blind and partially sighted.*

3.   *Local charities and organizations that help the blind and disabled.*

4.   *Those who are blind to God's love for them.*

(After each bidding the candle is lit by a helper. When the prayers are completed the candles could be placed in a holder or on the altar or a side table.)

Final hymn   'Come sing the praise of Jesus' (HTC 208) or 'Thou, whose almighty word' (HON 514)

The blessing or grace

Donald Dowling

The blind man's story

This retelling of the story of the healing of the blind man lends itself to dramatization. The teller can enter with a white stick, dark glasses and a begging bowl, sit down in front of the congregation and tell his story. He can then mime the appropriate points of his story, such as the anointing of his eyes, washing his face in the pool, his amazement at receiving his sight (throwing away his stick, glasses and bowl), his puzzlement at the reactions to the miracle, his second encounter with Jesus, etc.

'Look at that beggar,' one of them said. I pretended not to hear. I've got used to being spoken about as if I wasn't there. When you're blind, people often treat you as if you are stupid or without feeling. 'Whose fault is it,' the voice went on, 'that he is blind? His or his parents'?'

I'd heard this kind of talk before, though it still hurt. I was born blind. How could I have done something to deserve it? As for my parents, it was hard enough for them to cope with my handicap, without being burdened with the guilt that somehow God was punishing them for their sins. And those who thought this way were more likely to kick or curse me than drop me a coin. They felt they were simply underlining God's verdict.

I started to shuffle off. No charity here, I thought, just another religious argument that might be followed by a blow or the deliberate knocking over of my begging bowl. Then I stopped. 'Neither this man nor his parents are to blame. He's here to show the glory of God.' It wasn't just the words – it was the voice. When you are blind you become something of an expert at voices. It was warm and compassionate. This man really cared. He wasn't a local; no, he came from the north, a working man by the sound of him, yet his words carried a note of authority. It must be Jesus. I'd heard about him. Who hadn't? A healer, a preacher, some even said a troublemaker. Others called him a prophet, a man of God.

Then he spoke to me – not about me, but to me. He sat down by my side. 'I'm going to put a paste on your eyes.' Just mud and spit, it was. 'I want you to go to the pool by the gate and wash it off.' Then I knew I'd reached a turning point in my life. This was the moment. I would see God's glory at work. So I went.

At the pool I bent down and splashed the water over my eyes. And I could see! Colour, shape and light came bursting in upon my brain. I got up and for a moment I was dazed and amazed. Then I yelled, 'I can see! I can see!' I danced and laughed, still shouting. Some mothers whipped their children away – they thought I was crazy. But I didn't care. I rushed back to my pitch, my laughter bringing tears to my eyes. I knew I must thank Jesus, but when I got there he'd gone.

I'm well known in this part of town, part of the scenery you could say. But some of my neighbours couldn't believe it. I must be somebody else. Others knew it was me, even if they were flabbergasted. You could imagine it soon reached the ears of the local religious leaders.

Oh, I forgot to mention that the day it happened was the Sabbath, like your Sunday only much stricter. There were rules metres long saying what you could and couldn't do on a Sabbath day. These leaders weren't as interested in my healing – they clearly disbelieved me – as in the fact that Jesus had broken the Sabbath rules. He'd worked on a day of rest. I couldn't care a hoot personally, all I knew was that I was blind but now I could see.

They called my parents. They were clearly scared and embarrassed. They had to admit that I was their son and that I was born blind, but they didn't want to give any credit to Jesus. They knew I'd be thrown out of the synagogue if they did. Those leaders really hated Jesus. I think they were jealous. 'Ask him,' my parents said, 'he's an adult.' You'd think I had caught some dreadful disease rather than been cured of my blindness.

But I wouldn't be put down. I told them what had happened and that I believed God was at work in Jesus. So let God sort out the breaking of the Sabbath. The fact was that I could now see, so why keep asking the same questions? Could it be that they wanted to follow Jesus too? At that they threw me out of the synagogue. They didn't like ordinary folk questioning their rules. I was upset. You'd think these people would be delighted at such a miracle. I certainly was. But they just could not see the wonder of it.

Soon afterwards Jesus found me again. I now saw him for the first time. One gaze was enough. I knew he was someone who was genuine, someone worth following, even worth being chucked out of the synagogue for. He asked me if I believed in the Son of man. I didn't understand the question at first, but when he explained that he was talking about himself, then what could I say but yes? He'd changed my life.

Donald Dowling

Become like a child

An all-age service

Bible reference

Mark 10.13-16

Preparation

- Invite as many children as possible to have their outlines or impressions drawn onto a large-scale frieze. The addition of names and/or words of praise from their mouths would be helpful. Invite as many adults as possible to do the same on a separate frieze.

- Prepare some large cards with the words suggested after the reading from Mark below. Have a supply of about ten spare cards and a thick felt-tipped pen ready too.

- Invite two or three individuals of different ages to come to the service prepared to respond to the question, 'What childlike characteristics are important for seeing and receiving God's love?' (See below.)

- Invite an all-age group to write prayers which emphasize trust, enthusiasm, forgiveness, direct-speaking and other 'childlike' qualities, and which focus on celebration and need in the world, the Church and the local community.

Welcome and introductory sentence 'Today I tell you, whoever does not receive the kingdom of God as a little child will never enter it' (Mark 10.15).

Hymn 'Will you come and follow me?' (HON 560, verses 1,4,5)

Have the frieze of the children, with as many children around it as possible, unfurled with a sense of ceremony. When it is unfurled have one person say, 'To such as these the kingdom of God belongs.' And then have all the children call out, 'The kingdom of God belongs to us!'

Talk Today we are considering why Jesus seemed to think that being like children was such good news.

Hymn 'Open our eyes, Lord' (MP 545; HON 409)

Reading Mark 10.13-16

Talk There are some important words in this reading.

Have each of the words written on the large pieces of card mentioned in the preparation session, and have them displayed as they are said.

'Bringing'   'touch'   'sternly'   'indignant'

'belongs'

'receive'   'child'   'blessed'

Hear the reading again and listen for the words.

This account is very important: Jesus says that everyone has to be like children in order to belong to God's kingdom. Several people have been thinking what it is about children that gives us a key to the kingdom. What childlike characteristics are so important for seeing and receiving God's love?

People of different ages share their responses to this question, hopefully bringing out words like: 'openness', 'inquisitiveness', 'straight-forwardness', 'enthusiasm', 'trust', 'anticipation', 'receptiveness', 'forgiveness'.

Hymn 'The word of God' (JP 474)

The peace

Prayers   *A suggested versicle (V) and response (R) for the prayers which have been prepared as described in the preparation section:*

Lord, we bring before you all the children in **the world**

The prayer

V   Help us to expect your love, O Lord

R   And to respond with eagerness and trust.

Lord, we bring before you your children in **the church**

The prayer

V   Help us to expect your love, O Lord

R   And to respond with eagerness and trust.

Lord, we bring before you your children in **this community**

The prayer

V   Help us to expect your love, O Lord

R   And to respond with eagerness and trust.

Hymn   'Lord of all hopefulness' (HON 313)

Talk   Our prayers have shown us that people of all ages have those childlike qualities which are so important for seeing and receiving God's love. So let's celebrate that.

(Unfurl the frieze again, then the frieze with the adults' outlines / impressions.)

Together we all say, **'To such as these . . . the kingdom of God belongs!'**

The blessing

Hymn   'Walk in the light' (HON 494; MP 664)

Judith Sadler

Passion/Easter
Doing the donkey work

Jesus sometimes gave his disciples bizarre instructions. Here Dave Hopwood explores what it might have been like for two disciples as they followed one of his more peculiar requests.

Bible references

Matthew 21.1-6

Mark 11.1-12

Luke 19.28-36

Cast

Peter, Andrew, Marcus

(*Scene: Peter and Andrew are walking into town.*)

Peter   You're not serious.

Andrew   That's what he said.

Peter   No, he didn't.

Andrew   What do you mean, no he didn't? You weren't even there.

Peter   All right then, but what's he want it for?

Andrew   Riding into town. What else do you think?

Peter   Well, it's cheaper I suppose.

Andrew   Oh, we're not paying for it.

Peter   I beg your pardon?

Andrew   We're just to collect the animals and if anyone asks . . .

Peter   They fell off the back of a lorry.

Andrew   (*Laughs*) No . . . he said to just tell them he needs them.

Peter   Oh! Oh, of course. And I suppose we can just pick up a couple of new suits, a three-piece suite and a trolley of shopping while we're at it.

Andrew   No, we haven't got time. But with the animals, we just say, 'The master needs them.'

Peter   The master needs them.

Andrew   There you are, you've got it already.

Peter   Andrew, have you ever heard of stealing? Only this largely resembles it. Oh, oh, look out! Here comes that headbanger from town. Ignore him. Don't look him in the eyes or he'll break your legs.

(*Enter Marcus, a rather hefty thug.*)

Andrew   Ah, hello.

Peter   Sshh! What are you doing?

Andrew   We've come for your animals.

Marcus   Oh, have you!

Peter   Oh no, no, no – course not.

Andrew   Yes we have. We're taking them with us.

Marcus   Oh? Anything else you want, like a knuckle sandwich?

Peter	No, not really. He was just having you on. We're just . . . browsing.
Andrew	Hang on. We were told to fetch your donkeys.
Marcus	Oh! Well, why didn't you say so in the first place?
Peter	You mean, we can have them?
Marcus	NO! Now clear off.
Peter	Ah, fine, super, can't argue with that then. Have a nice day . . .
Andrew	But . . . the master needs them.
Peter	You keep out of this.
Marcus	The master?
Peter	Sorry to bother you. We'll be off now, don't worry too much about Andrew here . . .
Marcus	Are you talking about that prophet from Galilee?
Peter	Yes, d'you know him?
Marcus	He took my son's packed lunch away.
Andrew	Did he? Oh dear, I am sorry . . .
Marcus	(*Smiling*) I'm not. He gave him twelve baskets of bread and fish in return. These animals, you said? Sure, have them. If he wants them . . .
Peter	Really? Thanks. He's going to ride into town on them.
Marcus	You're joking. On those? I can let you have my best horse for him. I've got the best in town here, better than anything the Roman officers can get.
Peter	Great idea . . .
Andrew	No thanks.
Peter	What? But think of the splash he could make with a good horse . . . centre-page spread in the *Daily Israeli*.
Andrew	Come on, Peter. We'd better be off. I think he only wanted these. (*They leave Marcus.*)
Peter	Nice guy that. See, I told you it would be easy . . .
	(*They exit. Marcus exits alone, shaking his head and muttering.*)

Dave Hopwood

The day Jesus died

Bible references
Matthew 27.32-61
Mark 15.21-47
Luke 23.26-56
John 19.17-42

A group mime in the form of a series of still pictures. The group, at least four people, move into each picture and freeze until the next one. Children would find it easy to present.

It had been a long morning and the people were tired.

(*All lean, stand or sit in tired poses.*)

Some had been awake all night, waiting to see what would happen.

(*All rub eyes and stare.*)

Would Jesus die? Would he really be crucified? Some of the people were angry.

(*All look angry.*)

Some confused.

(*Look confused.*)

Some were afraid, while others were very unhappy.

(*Look frightened and sad.*)

Just before midday they saw him – Jesus – looking so terrible. They hardly recognized him.

(*Look shocked and turn away, or hide behind each other.*)

The disciples were shocked, the women wept, the children ran for their lives.

(Some show shock, others cry, others start to run away.)

The soldiers led Jesus out. They took him up through the streets, carrying a huge, awful cross. His back was all scarred, his face beaten, and on his head there was a crown of thorns.

(One becomes Jesus, carrying an imaginary cross. The others are soldiers, pushing and grabbing him.)

Up the hill they led him, to a place where two thieves were already dying.

(Two of the group become thieves on either side, in cross positions. Others remain as crowd or soldiers with Jesus.)

They threw him to the ground and hammered, hammered, hammered his wrists onto the wood. And they smashed his body against that cross.

(Soldiers nail Jesus to imaginary cross on floor. Others watch.)

The people gasped as they saw him lifted up. Jesus, the Son of God, raised high – but not on a throne, on a cross of agony, so that everyone could see him die.

(Soldiers stand Jesus up in cross position. Others look on.)

There would be no doubt that the Messiah was dead.

(Crowd take up different positions, playing cards, weeping, laughing, talking, staring.)

Three long hours he hung in pain, looking down and forgiving those who laughed, those who scoffed, those who betrayed and doubted, those who killed him. You and me.

(All turn and stare suddenly at the cross.)

For three long hours he looked at us, until he had no more love left in him. He had poured it all out.

And then he died.

(Jesus dies. All bury their heads and turn away.)

He gave up his life. He did it for you and me. And then they took him down.

(All gather round Jesus and take his body down.)

And they sealed his body in a borrowed tomb.

(All form a covering over the top so that Jesus is hidden.)

For he had nowhere of his own to lay his head. There was still no room in the world.

(All freeze.)

Dave Hopwood

Follow the way

An Easter all-age service

This service requires:
A leader plus at least four actors and a reader
Two large bundles of books
Road signs – and optionally paper and pens
Easel and board or other display stand
Rucksack
Small table and three chairs

Hymn	'All creatures of our God and King' (HAMNS 105)
Leader	Let us pray.
	Father, we have come to your house today to worship you,
	to give thanks to you for all your goodness,
	and to share with you our hopes and needs;
	help us to know that you are here now,
	and that you remain with us always. Amen.

(Chris comes on wearing a rucksack. Actor 1 and Actor 2 line up off stage ready to come and speak to him.)

Leader	Now here's someone who looks like he's going somewhere. Are you just off on a hike?
Chris	No, it's been a long journey and I'm going home.
Leader	Has it been an interesting trip?
Chris	Yes, very interesting. The experience of a lifetime, you could say.
Leader	Do you mind telling me your name?
Chris	Not at all – it's Chris Pilgrim. Chris, short for Christian.
Leader	Well, Chris, it was good to meet you. Have a safe journey, and a happy one!
Chris	Thank you. I'm sure I will.
	(He marches on the spot. Actor 1 approaches carrying a large bundle of books.)

Actor 1	Hello, traveller. Isn't this a nice day?
Chris	Yes, indeed. One of God's most beautiful days.
Actor 1	God? You don't believe in God, do you?
Chris	Of course I do. Look at this wonderful world – and at you and me! Who else but God could have made all this?
Actor 1	Huh! A load of nonsense! This world is just an accident, a freak of nature – and so are you. Here, let me give you one or two books to read. They should soon convince you that religion is a lot of twaddle. (*Hands over bundle to Chris, who staggers with the weight. Actor 1 goes off.*)
Chris	Oh dear. Oh dear, oh dear, oh dear. I wonder if she's right? Perhaps there is no God after all. If that's true, then my whole journey has been wasted. I don't feel like going on.
Actor 2	(*Approaching with another bundle of books.*) My, my, you look down in the dumps. What's the matter with you, my friend?
Chris	I just feel unhappy and fed up. Life seems to have lost its purpose. I don't know what to believe any more.
Actor 2	Ah, so you're a Christian then?
Chris	Yes, Christian's my name, and I am a Christian too . . .or at least I was.
Actor 2	We can't have this. You should be happy and smiling all the time if you're a Christian. Look, I've got some books that will show you how wrong you are to be sad and full of doubt. Here, have them. (*Hands over bundle and goes off. Chris staggers and has to put the bundles down.*)
Chris	(*Begins to cry*) Oh, this is awful. (*Sob*) Now I don't know what to believe (*sob*) and I feel so guilty!
	(*Christ approaches.*)
Christ	Can I help? Would you like to tell me about it?
Chris	I . . . I'm so sad and upset. A few minutes ago I was happy. I was on my way home, or so I thought. But then I met two people who have weighed me down with doubts and guilty feelings . . . and I don't think I can go on.
Christ	Well, I might be able to help a bit. You see, I've had my doubts too, but I've found that every Christian has *some* doubts, and doubt isn't the opposite of faith. Doubt is the opposite of being certain.
Chris	So you can have doubts and still be a Christian?

Christ	Yes. Faith is faith, not certainty.
Chris	Well, I suppose so . . .
Christ	And I don't think *anyone* can be happy and smiling all the time – not even a Christian. So there's no need to feel guilty.
Chris	I never thought of that.
Christ	Right then, Chris. Drop those stupid books right here, and go on your way.
	(*Chris puts down parcels, and sets off. Then he turns back.*)
Chris	Hey . . . how did you know my name?
Christ	Because I know you and everyone, Chris. I am the one who suffered and died to set you free from everything that weighs you down, or comes between you and God. (*Quickly turns and walks off.*)
Chris	(*Pauses, thinks, looks at congregation, then turns.*) JESUS! Wait! Let me come with you. (*Hurries off after Christ.*)
Hymn	'Father, hear the prayer we offer' (HAMNS 113) (*during this hymn a table and three chairs are put in the middle and the books are removed*).
Leader	Remember Chris Pilgrim, our traveller? Well, he's set off on his journey again, but this time he knows that he is walking with Jesus. We'll catch up with him again later. But look, coming along the road now are two more travellers (*Actor 1 and Actor 2 come on*) and they don't look too happy either.
Actor 2	It's a long way to Emmaus, isn't it?
Actor 1	I think it just seems longer today because we're so upset.
Actor 2	Yes, I thought Jesus was going to be the one who would drive out the Romans at last, and give us back our own land.
Actor 1	And instead he ends up dying on a cross. Oh, it's so unfair. He never did anyone any harm! (*Christ comes and joins them.*)
Christ	Do you mind if I walk with you?
Actor 2	No, we could do with a bit of company.
Christ	Yes, you two *have* got long faces. What's the matter?
Actor 1	Are you the only one who hasn't heard about what happened to Jesus of Nazareth? We were his followers, and we expected him to do great things, but instead he ended up being killed.

Actor 2   Except that some of our friends say they have seen him alive again.

Actor 1   And that's a likely story, isn't it?

Christ   Your trouble is that you don't know your Scriptures very well. Jesus *had* to suffer and die like that. It was the only way he could win the battle with evil. There are all kinds of hints and clues in the Scriptures about Jesus dying, if you know where to look. Read the prophets, and see what they have to say.

Actor 2   (*Pointing*) Look, we're nearly there. There's Emmaus.

Actor 1   It's going to be dark soon. Why don't you stop and have a meal with us?

Actor 2   And maybe stay the night?

Christ   Yes, thank you, I'd like that.

（*They sit down at the table.*）

Actor 2   Everything's ready for supper. Would you say grace and bless our meal, stranger?

（*Actor 2 and Actor 1 bow their heads as Christ speaks.*）

Christ   Blessed be the God and Father of us all, who gives us bread to eat and wine to drink. Blessed be his name!

（*Christ gets up and goes off.*）

**Actors
1 and 2**   (*Look up astonished, pause, look at each other, then turn to the empty chair and say:*) JESUS!

Leader   (*Off stage*) But he had vanished.

Actor 2   Come on, let's go.

Actor 1   Where to?

Actor 2   Back to Jerusalem, of course. We've got to tell everybody that we've seen the Lord!

（*Actors 1 and 2 go off.*）

Leader   Because Jesus came back to life again at Easter on a Sunday, Sunday has always been the most important day of the week for those who follow him. But it's also important because it's the day of the week when the story of creation says that God rested from his work — which is why we have it as a day for rest and enjoyment. And it's the day when the Holy Spirit first came to the followers of Jesus. So Sunday is important three times over. Now we're going to sing a song about it:

Song   'This is the day' (HON 508)

(Actor 1 and Actor 2 put out board, easel road signs and pen. Table and chairs are removed. Actor 1 stays by easel but Actor 2 goes to centre and is joined by Chris.)

Chris   Help! I'm trying to learn the Highway Code. What do all these road signs mean?

Actor 2   There are signs which tell you which way to go . . .

Actor 1   *(Pointing to first sign – a direction sign)* Like 'Turn off at the next junction for the A 684'.

Actor 2   And signs that warn you of hazards ahead . . .

Actor 1   *(Revealing next sign)* Like a 'hump-backed bridge' *(reveals next sign)* or a 'double bend'. *(Removes last sign to reveal blank triangle.)*

Chris   So basically signs tell me which way to go, and they help me get there safely?

Actor 2   That's right. There are a few more complications, but you won't go far wrong if you know that.

              (Chris and Actor 2 go off.)

Leader   Listen to this reading and see if you can work out the connection between what happens in the reading and a journey everyone has to make.

Reader   This reading comes from the Gospel of John.

              Jesus said to his friends, 'Don't worry. Just trust in God and trust in me. There is lots of room in God's house. If that were not true, would I have told you that I am going there to make everything ready for you? Then I shall come back for you, so that you can be with me. And you already know how to get there.'

              Thomas said to him, 'Lord, we don't know where you are going, so how can we know the way?'

              Jesus answered, 'I am the way, and the truth, and the life. People can only find the way to God by following me.'

Leader   So Jesus told his friends that *he* was the way through life – and he still is. And what sort of way is it if we follow him?

              (Actor 1 draws or reveals a 'road narrows' sign.)

              What does that sign mean?

              (Answers from congregation.)

Jesus told us that the right way through life is narrow and quite hard. Listen to what he said:

Reader   'Go in by the narrow gate. It's a wide gate that leads the wrong way; there's plenty of room on that road, and many people choose that way. But the gate that leads the right way is small; the road is narrow, and few people find it.'

Leader   If we go the wrong way – if we don't follow Jesus – then these are the sorts of signs we might see on that road:

(*Actor 1 draws or reveals a 'steep hill down' sign.*)

What does that sign mean?

(*Answers from congregation.*)

Yes – very easy to go down, but steep and dangerous, and it's easy to lose control of your car or bike and have a crash.

(*Actor 1 draws or reveals a 'slippery road' sign.*)

And what about this sign? What does this mean?

(*Answers from congregation.*)

The easy way is also slippery. Once you start skidding you can't stop and you end up hurting yourself or somebody else. That happens when we don't follow Jesus too – we get hurt; other people get hurt; and all because of the wrong things we do. But the right way isn't easy. It's not just a narrow road, it's this as well:

(*Actor 1 draws or reveals a 'steep hill up' sign.*)

What does that mean?

(*Answers from congregation.*)

So the journey of life can feel like an uphill struggle at times. It's so easy to do bad things, and so hard to do the right things.

(*Chris returns with the rucksack on his back, followed by Christ. Actor 1 goes off.*)

Leader   Now look – here's our friend Chris Pilgrim again. He looks a lot older. But then he would, for many years have passed.

Chris   (*Putting down his rucksack*) Well, Jesus, I'm nearly home now. It's been a long journey, and a hard one at times.

Christ   Yes it has. But I never promised you that life would be easy. I only promised to be with you always, whatever happened and wherever you went.

Chris   Yes, but when I look back at our tracks, sometimes I can only see one set of footprints, not two. So how can you say that you were always there?

Christ   Chris, that was when your way was hardest, and there's only one set of footprints there because that's when I was carrying you.

Chris   (*Pause*) Thank you, Jesus. That's all I need to know.

(*Christ picks up the rucksack and helps Chris off.*)

Song   'The journey of life' (BBC CP 45)

Leader   (*Actor 1 and Actor 2 return.*)

On our journey through life we shall meet all kinds of obstacles and pick up all kinds of things which weigh us down and spoil our friendship with God and with each other. There will be changes and problems, hard decisions to make, and many sad 'goodbyes'. But we must remember that Jesus has promised to be with us always:

Actor 1   Wherever we go

Actor 2   whatever we do

Actor 1   in good times

Actor 2   and in bad times.

Leader   And Jesus knows how hard the way is. He knows about pain, and being tempted to do wrong – and about what it's like to die. So that's why he's the best guide and travelling companion we can have in life.

Now our prayers. Let us pray:

Let's be very quiet and still for a few moments as we listen to some soft music, and in our hearts let's bring to God the problems of the world, our own problems, and everything which makes the journey of life harder.

(*Pause. Music: Kyrie from Vaughan Williams'* Mass in G minor *or other suitable piece.*)

Lord, our hearts are heavy with sadness as we see people fighting and killing.

(*Pause.*)

Lord, we pray for your peace.

Lord, we feel the weight of pain and suffering as some people are sick, and others were born with problems which hinder them on their journey.

(*Pause.*)

Lord, we ask your help for them.

Lord, we have problems too; secrets that only you and we know, and things that everybody can see.

(*Pause.*)

Lord, forgive us where we have been wrong and help us to carry the burdens we cannot put down.

(*Pause, then fade music.*)

We ask all these things for the sake of Jesus, our Saviour. **Amen**.

Actor 1	God of every age and people,
Actor 2	God of all who travelled your way in the past,
Actor 1	And all who walk your path today.
Actor 2	Help us to be true Christian pilgrims.
Actor 1	May we find the right road
Actor 2	And not be tempted to go astray.
Actor 1	May we take Jesus as our guide and companion
Actor 2	And help others on their journey through life.
Actor 1	And lead us at last to the home you have prepared for us. **Amen**.

Hymn   'Thine be the glory' (HAMNS 428)

The blessing

Don Tordoff

The hill

Bible reference

Matthew 28.16-20

One evening, in a country in a land far away, a group of friends were sitting together on a hill. They looked out over the town below them and watched people returning home after working in the fields all day. The sun was setting and the wind was blowing softly through the trees on the hillside. It was starting to get cold so the friends lit a fire to keep themselves warm.

The friends were sitting on a hill because they had had a message. They had been told to go there to wait for someone, someone whom they knew very well. They knew him well because they had spent three years with him. They had lived, eaten, travelled, learned and worked with him. Sometimes they had all argued and fallen out with each other, but they were all still friends. They were like brothers, even though they didn't all belong to the same family.

But three days ago, they had seen this friend killed. They had seen him die with their own eyes, and they had all been very sad. They didn't know what they should do. Some of them thought that they should forget about their friend and go back to work as fishermen. Some thought that they should hide away in case they got into trouble because of the things their friend had said when he'd been alive. All of them were very sad.

Then today they had heard that their friend wasn't really dead. Some women had told them that their friend was alive and that he had told them to come to this hill to wait for him. Now what would you think if you heard that? What would you think if you had seen someone die, and then heard that he was alive again? What do you think the friends thought? Well, they were confused. They were mixed up. They felt like they were dreaming and when they pinched themselves they found that they were very much awake. So, was it true? Was their friend alive? Just imagine if he was.

After a while some of the friends began to say, 'He's not coming. I told you he wasn't going to come. Let's go back to our boats and carry on fishing.'

Some said, 'Well, let's wait a little while longer – perhaps until the sun has set – and then we'll go.' You see, they wanted to stay just in case it was true. Some said, 'He'll come. Remember what he told us when we were with him. He always talked about coming back to life. Just be patient.'

About an hour later, after the sun had set and the stars had begun to appear in the purple-blue sky, the friends heard a noise on the hillside. 'It could just be a goat,' said someone.

'It could be him!' said another. They waited to see if the noise would get louder, and it did. Whoever it was was coming closer.

Then they saw him. It was their friend Jesus. Some of the friends immediately fell at his feet and told him how much they loved him and how happy they were to see him alive. They cried with happiness, they laughed, they danced and sang and they praised Jesus because they realized that he was God's special Son. Some of the friends, however, were not so sure. They still couldn't believe that this was Jesus, so they stayed back and didn't go near him.

When everyone was calm again, Jesus came near to them and told them that he was now in charge of everything in the world and in heaven and now he had a job for his friends to do.

'Go to all the countries in the world and tell people about me,' he said. 'Tell people how I was killed, but have come back to life, and show people how to follow me. Tell them all the things I taught you about God and about how to live a new life.'

When the friends heard this they were excited, but they were also worried. How could they go and tell people about Jesus? There were only a few of them and there were thousands of people in the world. How could they even tell just one town about Jesus? The ones who were most worried, however, were the ones who had thought that this man wasn't really Jesus. How could they go and tell people? They hadn't even believed that Jesus was really alive again. Perhaps Jesus would tell them off and be angry with them for not believing him. They felt like they had let Jesus down.

But then Jesus said to all his friends, including the ones who doubted him, 'I will always be with you, to the end of time.'

Then they were really excited, because they knew that they would be able to go and tell people about who Jesus was because they would not be going on their own – Jesus would be going with them.

Simon Marshall

Easter card

You will need:

White card or stiff white paper
Cartridge paper
Fibre-tip pens or wax crayons
Scissors
Glue stick

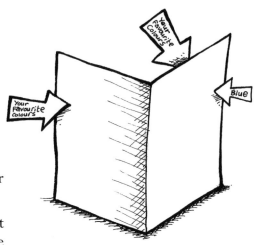

Bend the white card or stiff white paper in two.

On the outside colour the card bright blue like the sky in spring. On the inside colour it with all your favourite colours.

Draw the two broken egg shapes, copying or tracing the drawing.

Colour in your two broken egg shapes and cut them out.

Glue them to the card, one high above the other.

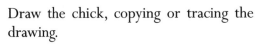

Draw the chick, copying or tracing the drawing.

Colour in your chick and cut it out carefully.

Draw a thin strip and colour it in your favourite colours.

Cut out the strip of paper and fold it backwards and forwards into a zigzag.

Glue the chick to the lower egg shape.

Draw lines from the top egg shape to the bottom, so it looks as if the chick is flying in a parachute.

If you want to, write: FLY HIGH AT EASTER somewhere on the card.

Add a bible verse inside on the theme of Christ bringing new life and freedom (such as John 3.16, Galatians 3.28 or 1 John 3.16).

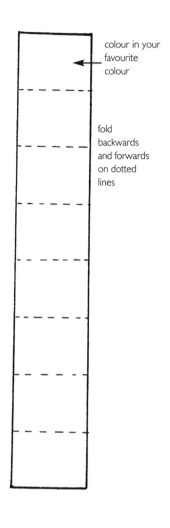

colour in your favourite colour

fold backwards and forwards on dotted lines

Susan Skinner

Pentecost

That's the Spirit

An imagined meeting between Simon Peter and two police officers in Jerusalem on the fateful Day of Pentecost.

Bible reference

Acts 2

Cast

Peter, Police Officers A and B

Props
Table, three chairs, tape-recorder

(Scene: It is lunch-time on the Day of Pentecost in Jerusalem. The two police officers are sitting behind the table. Peter is seated in front of them. He is full of energy and enthusiastic throughout, leaping up and down from time to time. The tape-recorder is on the table.)

Officer A *(Switching on the tape-recorder)* Interview with one Simon Peter, Jerusalem, Day of Pentecost.

Officer B *(To Peter)* You are Simon Peter?

Peter Correct.

Officer B From Galilee?

Peter Correct again.

Officer B Occupation?

Peter Fisherman. Well, ex. Now I fish for men.

Officer B *(To A)* What is he talking about?

Officer A *(To B)* Look, don't expect to make sense of all this. Just ask the questions.

Officer B All right. *(To Peter)* Well, sir, we've had a few complaints about disturbances in the city this morning. I should explain, you're not under arrest or anything. We just wanted to check up on what's going on.

Officer A There are a lot of people out there who are a bit confused . . .

Officer B Bewildered . . .

Officer A Perplexed . . .

Officer B Stunned . . .

Peter *(Getting carried away)* Excited, amazed, challenged, thrilled?

Officer B *(Grudgingly)* Well, yes. Some of them. Not all. We had some people in from Macedonia . . .

Officer A Some from Cappadocia . . .

Officer B Some from Pamphylia . . .

Officer A Some from Egypt . . .

Officer B Jews . . .

Officer A Non-Jews . . .

Officer B Cretans . . .

Officer A Arabs . . .

Peter Parthians, Medes, Elamites, Libyans . . . Never seen so many visitors in the city. What a fantastic opportunity. Today of all days! It's brilliant timing, isn't it?

Officer A (*To B*) As I said, don't expect to make sense of all this.

Officer B Well the thing is, sir, all these foreign visitors said that when you and your lads started speaking this morning, it was as though they were all hearing you talking in their own language.

Peter Yes . . .

Officer B Well, it's a bit . . . spooky, isn't it?

Officer A A bit weird.

Officer B Perplexing.

Officer A Bewildering.

Peter (*Getting carried away again*) Miraculous! Amazing! Stunning! Exciting!

Officer B Yes, all right, sir. Just calm down, will you?

Officer A And then we've had these reports that when you spoke to the crowd, you claimed that the teacher Jesus of Nazareth . . .

Officer B Whom we ourselves saw crucified, dead and buried, in this very city, only seven weeks ago . . .

Officer A Was alive again! Is this true?

Peter It certainly is!

Officer B What, true that you said it?

Peter Correct.

Officer B Or true that it happened?

Peter Correct again!

Officer B So, what exactly did you say about this Jesus that got them all so excited this morning?

Peter Well, I just reminded them first of all that they had seen and heard for themselves the miraculous things Jesus did and the amazing things he said.

Officer A Well, yes. That is true. We did see the signs.

Peter	And that these all testified quite clearly that he was at least a man sent from God.

Officer B	But he was arrested, and found guilty of something or other, I'm not sure what.

Peter	(*Getting more and more excited*) But that was all in God's purposes! All in his great plan of salvation! Your lot took him off and put him to death by nailing him on a cross. But then God raised him to life again to prove that he was the Christ, the Son of the living God! Isn't that amazing? Isn't that stunning? Exciting? Miraculous? God has raised this Jesus to life. And I and all the others, well, we're witnesses to it. We've seen him. Spoken to him. Eaten with him. He's shown us how all his sufferings and now his rising again were all foretold in the Scriptures. (*Now standing on his chair and speaking as though addressing a crowd*) Let all Israel be assured of this: God has made this Jesus, whom you crucified, both Lord and Christ!

Officer A	Yes, all right, sir. Er, just calm down, will you?

Peter	(*Sitting down again*) Well, anyway, that's what I was telling them this morning.

Officer A	I see. Now, there is just one thing I don't quite get.

Officer B	(*To A*) Just one thing?

Officer A	(*To B*) Well, several actually, but let's try this one. (*To Peter*) Am I right in thinking, sir, that you are the same Simon Peter from Galilee who was overheard in Jerusalem on the morning before Passover denying three times that you even knew this Jesus of Nazareth?

Peter	Correct.

Officer B	And was later seen outside the temple courtyard crying like a three-year-old?

Peter	Correct again!

Officer A	Well, sir, how exactly do you explain it? The dramatic change, I mean. You don't appear to be the same person. What's happened to you that makes you stand up in the city this morning in front of all those crowds, apparently without any fear or trepidation, and boldly claim that this Jesus has risen from the dead?

Peter	(*A little embarrassed*) Um. That's the Spirit . . .

Officer B	Spirit! Some of them said they thought you were drunk. We had you down for a few too many glasses of Chateau Bethany. But it's spirits, is it?

Officer A   And only nine o'clock in the morning. Tut, tut! Disgraceful!

Peter   No, what I meant was . . .

Officer B   (*Producing a breathalyser*) I'm sorry, sir. But I shall have to ask you to breathe into this.

   (*Peter does so. The officer examines it and is puzzled.*) Mmm. Zero! (*To A*) Steroids?

Peter   Look, I'm not drunk! I'm not on drugs! (*Getting excited again*) What's happened is simply what   was foretold by the prophet Joel. God has poured out his Holy Spirit on us.

Officer B   Oh, the Holy Spirit!

   (*From this point on the two officers begin to be more sympathetic and interested.*)

Peter   Yes! God has raised Jesus to life. Exalted to the right hand of God, Jesus has received from the Father the promised Holy Spirit and has poured him out on all of us who believe in him. That's what's happened to us this morning.

Officer A   Well, I suppose that could explain it all . . .

Officer B   But that would mean that Jesus . . .

Officer A   I know, but there has to be some explanation. Look, Simon Peter, maybe what you say is true . . .

Officer B   Maybe this Jesus of yours is risen from the dead . . .

Officer A   But if it is all true, what do we do?

Officer B   Yes, tell us. What do we do?

Peter   (*Standing and opening his arms in invitation*) Repent, and be baptized in the name of Jesus Christ for the forgiveness of your sins. And you too will receive the gift of the Holy Spirit. And this promise is not just for you (*gesturing towards the audience*) but for all whom the Lord our God will call, both here and far off, both now and in the years to come!

Derek Haylock

Wind, fire . . . and a whisper in your ear

An all-age service for Pentecost which uses modern and traditional ideas to convey a sense of the Holy Spirit's power and love.

Bible reference

Acts 2.1-41

Welcome and introduction

Hymn 'Come down, O Love divine (HAMNS 156)' or 'There's a spirit in the air' (HAMNS 515)

Optional introductory prayer and confession

Leader Let us pray . . .

Dear God, help us feel and know that you are near us.

Open our ears to hear your voice;

our mouths to sing and speak your praise;

and our hearts to receive your love.

Amen.

Let us be quiet and still for a moment and think of the ways in which we have failed to be and to do all that God wants.

Heavenly Father,

we have done wrong things,

thought wrong things,

and failed to do all that we should.

Forgive us now, we pray,

and help us to begin again.

Amen.

Talk

Leader   Today we are going to begin by thinking about the wind.

We can't see the wind, can we, but we can see and feel what the wind does. Can you suggest some ways in which we might *feel* the wind? (*The breeze on our faces, the strong push or pull of a gale. Try to make sure that the gentle effects of the wind are mentioned as well as the strong.*)

And how might we *see* the wind at work? (*A flag flapping in the breeze, smoke blowing away from chimneys, leaves blowing off a tree – or even the tree itself being blown down.*)

So the wind can be very gentle, and very strong too.

Helper   It certainly can! Even walking down the road on a windy day can be quite hard. (*Leader and helper mime walking through the wind, holding on to their hats.*)

Leader   Hold on to your hat. It might blow away.

Helper   Look at all the dead leaves rushing past us.

Leader   Ouch! The leaves and the twigs are hurting my legs.

Helper   This is a great day for flying a kite . . . (*mimes being dragged along and off to one side*) if you're strong enough!

Leader   So perhaps the best word we can use to describe the wind is POWERFUL. That doesn't just mean that it is strong – powerful things can be gentle too. But the wind has so much power that we can use it to help us. How do we make the wind work for us? (*Sailing ships, drying washing, windmills. The helper returns with a windmill – a child's toy one or some more elaborate model.*)

And we can use windmills to do all sorts of useful things. Can you tell us what a windmill will do?

Helper   It will grind corn to make flour. It will pump water to help crops grow. It will generate electricity for things like lights and televisions. Has anyone ever seen a wind farm, where there are lots of wind generators all together? (*Children in the congregation might be invited to make the windmill work by blowing hard.*)

Leader   The Bible describes the Holy Spirit as being like the wind, a powerful wind, or like the gentle breath of God. Let's sing a hymn asking God to breathe his life and his power gently into us.

Hymn   'Breathe on me, Breath of God' (HAMNS 157)

Leader We've thought a lot about wind. Now we're going to think about another powerful thing – FIRE. (*Light a candle from a match.*) Fire can be very dangerous, so we must be careful. We need to learn how to use fire safely. Then no one will get hurt.

Helper Fire spreads so quickly. A spark can start a forest fire, or someone being careless with a cigarette can burn down a building. Fire is powerful, just like the wind. And just like the wind we can use it to help us.

Leader Can you suggest ways in which we can use fire and heat to help us? (*Cook food. Boil water for washing up and a cup of tea. Keep our homes warm in winter. Heat furnaces to make metal, or generate electricity in a different way from a windmill.*)

WIND and FIRE are two of the most powerful things we know about. (*Hold up candle.*) Can you guess how I can use the power of the wind to overcome the power of the fire? (*Blow out candle – or invite one of the congregation to do it.*)

Today is the day we call 'Pentecost' or 'Whitsunday'. On this day we think about that special form of GOD'S power which we call the HOLY SPIRIT.

Helper Before Jesus went back to heaven, he told his followers what they must do when he had gone. He wanted them to go everywhere, and tell everyone about him, but that would often be hard and dangerous.

Leader Jesus knew that on their own they would not have the power to do it. So he told them to wait for a little while, and then they would be given all the power they needed. They would be given the power of God, the Holy Spirit, living and working inside them. That happened on the Day of Pentecost, fifty days after Easter.

This is how the Bible tells the story:

Reader On the Day of Pentecost, the followers of Jesus were sitting together in one room, when suddenly they heard the sound of a strong wind blowing right through the whole house, and they could see something like flames everywhere which came and touched each one of them. In this way they were all filled with the Holy Spirit.

At once they went outside and began to tell everyone the story of Jesus. There were people there from every part of the world and they were all able to understand the good news of what God had done in their own language (Acts 2.1–6).

143

Leader The Holy Spirit is someone we can't see, or touch, or hear. But we can feel him inside us, and see what he does through us and other people. That first Day of Pentecost must have been very exciting. Let's imagine that we have one of the disciples here now to tell us about it.

Disciple It was such a strange and wonderful experience that we were a bit stuck for words. We heard and we felt this rushing wind. Someone said it was like a gale blowing right through us. And when we saw what looked like flames around us, I felt such a wonderful warming of my heart, such a burning inside me, that I said it was like fire. But it wasn't a dangerous wind, or a fire which might harm us. It was power under control, power being used properly and safely.

Leader Power is no good on its own. We have to use it properly and safely – like a furnace uses fire or a windmill uses wind. (*Pick up a weather-vane – this may be a model, in which case it may be demonstrated – or a large drawing. In either case the NSEW indicators should be held on with Blutak.*)

Does anyone know what this is? Yes, a weather-vane. We see them on the tops of buildings, and they tell us what direction the wind is coming from. (*Demonstrate weather-vane if using a model.*) North, south,

east, west — when the wind blows we know its direction because the wind makes the arrow point the right way. When the Holy Spirit blows into us, he points us in the right direction, the way God wants us to go. He is God coming to us and pointing us *his* way. Listen in our second reading to some words Paul wrote long ago about this:

Reader What I say is this: Let the Holy Spirit direct your lives, then you will not want to do wrong or selfish things. We all want to go our way, which is the opposite of God's way. But if the Spirit leads you then you will be free to go God's was (Galatians 5.16-18).

Song 'Spirit of God' (SHF 486) or 'The Spirit lives to set us free' (HON 494)

Leader So the work of the Holy Spirit is to point us the right way. That happens to some people in the sort of amazing way that happened to the disciples on the Day of Pentecost. But it also happens in tiny ways, through the still small voice of God which seems to whisper in our ear, 'I am the way, follow me.'

And when the Spirit gives us a job to do, he also gives us the power we need to do it, just like he did for the first disciples. God wants to give power to all his people, including you and me, to go all over the world and tell everyone about Jesus.

People go to the north (*take the N and stick it on a large sheet of paper or world map*),

and to the east (*take the E and stick it on*),

and to the west (*take the W and stick it on*),

and to the south (*take the S and stick it on, then hold up sheet*),

so that the good news about Jesus will go to every part of the world. It is the power of God the Holy Spirit, working inside us, which helps us tell the news, and be like Jesus.

Prayers (*Conducted by the Leader or another person.*)

So now our prayers. To help us to pray we are going to use some quiet music. You may know the tune, because it's possibly the oldest hymn about the Holy Spirit we have in our hymn books. It's called 'Come Holy Ghost, our souls inspire', and it's the hymn we usually use when people are confirmed or ordained. (*This may be best played by a solo instrument, either live or a recording.*)

Spirit of God, you are strong as the wind, and gentle as a breath. Come and breathe into our hearts to make us fresh and clean. Blow away all that is cold and bad, and everything which hurts or harms us or other people. Come, Holy Spirit, come.

(*Leave space for people to pray.*)

Spirit of God, you are as powerful as fire. Come and warm our hearts and set us on fire with love for you and for all the world. Point us in the right direction, and give us the power we need to do your work. Come, Holy Spirit, come.

(*Leave space for people to pray.*)

Spirit of God, on the first Day of Pentecost people of all different nations and races heard the good news in their own languages. May your Church today be so filled with your power that it may speak to everyone, in ways they can understand, of the love you have for all men and women. Come, Holy Spirit, come.

(*Leave space for people to pray.*)

Spirit of God, you bring peace to human hearts and minds. Spread abroad your peace in the affairs of the world. Bless the efforts of those seeking to make and keep peace in the world's trouble spots, and guide those who are trying to rebuild the lives of communities and countries ravaged by war. Into all those places where peace is needed: Come, Holy Spirit, come.

(*Leave space for people to pray.*)

Spirit of God, your work is to bring healing to broken lives and sick minds. Bless with your presence and help the work of surgeons, doctors and nurses and make whole and well all those who are ill or in need. Come, Holy Spirit, come.

(*Leave space for people to pray.*)

Praise to your eternal merit. Father, Son and Holy Spirit.

Amen.

(*Fade out the music.*)

Hymn   'Gracious Spirit, Holy Ghost' (HON 184) or 'Father, Lord of all Creation' (HON 122)

Don Tordoff

Acts

A changed man

'Stachys, talk to me,' said my friend Matthias. 'What on earth has happened to Saul?'

'Saul?' I swallowed a large amount of wine.

'Saul, Saul of Tarsus. Your boss. Remember?'

Oh, I remembered all right. I shifted uncomfortably and hoped Matthias would offer me some more wine, but he didn't. He leaned towards me, interested. 'From what I hear, something's happened to him.'

I averted my gaze. Yes, Matthias was right. Something had happened to Saul of Tarsus. I'd been there with him when it had happened.

'One minute he's travelling about, arresting men and women who belong to that strange new sect, throwing them in prison – a man with a real mission in life – and the next minute . . .'

'Yes, yes, I know. All of a sudden he's joined with the very people he's been persecuting.'

'And not keeping quiet about it. You might say he's got a new mission in life. What happened, Stachys?'

'What happened?' I murmured, and I thought of Saul.

I'd worked with Saul of Tarsus for quite a while. He was a learned man, educated in religious knowledge, not like me. I think he took me along on his journeys because of my reputation as a fighting man, scared of nothing and no one – not even Romans. Saul wanted me, and a few others, to accompany him while he found out where his enemies were hiding. He called them 'disciples', people who were following the teaching of a carpenter from Nazareth, a man called Jesus. Saul hated the followers of Jesus. He wanted to kill them all. So I went along with him and helped him arrest these disciples.

'Perhaps we can get the leader,' I had suggested one day. 'If we made a spectacle of this Jesus they follow, maybe that would crush the whole sect.'

'Oh, he's already dead,' Saul had told me. 'He was crucified.'

'And yet they still follow him?'

'They're fanatics. One of them, called Stephen, spoke blasphemy before the High Priest and all the elders. He was put to death. I was there. I gave my approval.'

'But you say their leader was crucified? You mean, they're willing to die for someone who is already dead?'

'Oh, they don't believe he's dead. They say Jesus was the Messiah, the Saviour who was to come into the world, and they say that God raised this Jesus from the dead. What blasphemy! I swear we'll get every single one of them.' Saul had smiled a cruel smile, suddenly. 'I have got letters from the High Priest to the synagogues in Damascus. So we're going to see if there are any disciples there. We'll bring them back to Jerusalem to be punished.'

As I recalled that conversation I saw again the murderous look in his eyes.

'Come on, come on, Stachys. Tell me all.'

I glanced at the eager face of Matthias. 'Well, we were on our way to Damascus.'

'And?' He poured me more wine, and I sat back, trying to put the details of my adventure into words.

'It was about noon. There was a bright light, it flashed all around us. Saul fell to his face in the road. I heard a noise . . .'

'Go on, go on!'

'Well, Saul got up, opened his eyes . . . and he was blind. We led him by the hand into Damascus.' I opened my mouth to finish off the story, but I shut it again. Matthias would never believe the rest.

Matthias frowned. 'That's it?'

'That's it.' I finished my wine and got to my feet. 'I must go. I hope to see you again soon, my friend.'

'But that doesn't explain why Saul is now calling himself Paul and professes himself a follower of this dead carpenter.'

'I must go.' As I stepped out of his house onto the street, I breathed a sigh of relief. No, Matthias would never understand if I told the rest. After all, I didn't understand it myself.

We had taken the blind Saul to the house of Judas, on Straight Street. Saul dismissed me – he said he no longer needed my services, but I had some fondness for my master, and I went back to the house a few days later to see how he was.

To my surprise, Saul's sight had returned, and he told me that he was now a follower of Jesus of Nazareth. At first I thought he was joking, but Saul would never joke about such things. Then I thought it was part of some crafty plan to capture his enemies, but I soon saw that he meant what he said. He was sincere, but he was happy and laughing. I'd never seen him laugh before. In fact, I had never seen such joy in anyone's eyes as I saw in his.

'I'm a changed man, Stachys,' he said.

He certainly looked changed. It was as if he was a different person altogether. No more threats, or murderous looks. Just joy.

I shook my head. 'I don't understand. How have you, my master, now become one of the very fanatics you were trying to destroy? Perhaps that bright light and your temporary blindness have affected you.'

'They certainly have!' he chuckled. 'I know you saw a light and heard a noise on the road, but I saw and heard much more. The Lord Jesus Christ himself appeared to me and spoke to me. I know without a doubt that he really is the Son of God, that he was dead and is alive, and is the Saviour of the world.'

Now, as I glanced back at Matthias' house, I wondered what he would have made of Saul's words?. What did I make of them? Something told me to seek out Saul again, and question him further. For one thing I know for sure – since Saul of Tarsus claimed to have met Jesus, he's been a changed man.

Sheila Jacobs

Make it yourself

A quick and easy way to illustrate Paul's shipwreck.

Bible reference

Acts 27

You will need:

Paper and pens or crayons

Scissors

Paper fasteners

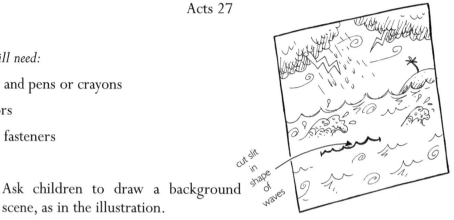

cut slit in shape of waves

1. Ask children to draw a background scene, as in the illustration.

2. On a separate piece of paper they are to draw a boat with a broken mast.

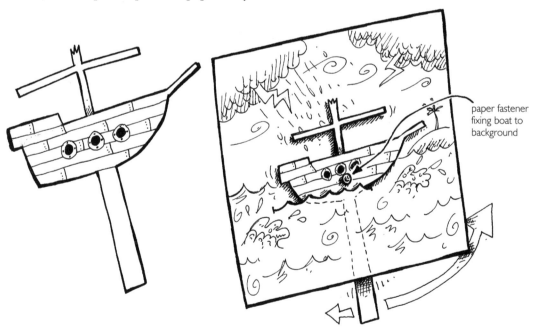

paper fastener fixing boat to background

3. Fasten the boat into the sea with a paper fastener. Now the children can tell the story of Paul and the shipwreck themselves.

Joy Blaylock

The people of God
An all-age service

This service is based on Acts 2.37-47 and aims to explore the following themes:

- *sharing together*
- *sharing in worship*
- *sharing with others.*

The structure is aimed to be as flexible as possible, and several alternative ideas are given wherever possible to help you adapt the material to your own church situation.

Welcome

Hymn 'Praise, my soul, the King of heaven' (HON)

Introductory sentence of Scripture 1 John 1.3

Introduction to the theme Being a Christian is about being part of God's community. You can't be a Christian alone. We all need to learn to work and share together. We also have to realize that we need each other.

Choose one of the following games to illustrate how we can learn to trust each other and work together.

1. Directions game

Place a bar of chocolate at the back of the church and then blindfold a member of the congregation. Use another volunteer to direct the blindfolded person to the chocolate.

2. Messy breakfast

You will need three adult or teenage volunteers for this game. Sit volunteer A on a chair in front of a table set for breakfast. Tell them that they are about to enjoy breakfast in church. The only disadvantage is that they have to have their hands tied behind their back and rely on another volunteer (B) to feed them! However, volunteer B is blindfolded and seated directly behind A, with arms around them. Volunteer C sits nearby and tells A what to do.

(This can be a very messy breakfast, especially if using cereal, milk and sugar, so be prepared. Maybe prime your volunteers well in advance.)

Reading   Acts 2.37-47

Song   'One shall tell another' (SHF 417)

1.   SHARING TOGETHER

'All the believers were together and had everything in common' (Acts 2.44).

Use one of the following methods to think about practical ways that we can share together:

(a)   Mime several situations where people could help each other – like sharing meals, baby-sitting, sharing gardening tools, celebrating birthdays – and get people to guess what you're doing. (*These need to be well rehearsed in advance.*)

(b)   Give out paper and pens. Ask both adults and children to draw one of the best ways they can think of to share together as a church. Stick these up on a board at the front of the church.

(c)   Have a simple brainstorming session about different ways of sharing, writing suggestions from the congregation on an overhead transparency.

Follow this discussion about sharing together with a very practical and, hopefully, delicious example of how it can be done.

Choose between five and ten members of the congregation, with a good mix of ages. Share out between them the ingredients from the recipe below. Make the point clear that each of the ingredients is useful, but it is only when they are mixed together that they can make really tasty results. In the same way, we are most effective in our Christian lives when we are sharing and working together, rather than going it alone.

Tell the group that you are setting them a difficult CHALLENGE that they must complete within twenty minutes. Give them the recipe and tell them that they must produce a 'chocolate slab' to be shared with all the church, and that all the team must be involved in its creation.

Song   'Let there be love' (SHF 318)

2.   SHARING IN WORSHIP

Confession   *Split this into three parts, confessing the times as* individuals, *the* Church, *and the* world, *that we fail to share and work together with others. Write out short sentences beforehand and give these to members of the congregation to read at the appropriate time.*

Worship in song   *This is an opportunity to allow for a longer time of sung worship together. The suggestions here offer the chance for a mixture between reflective and lively songs.*

Reflective

'A new commandment' (SHF 14)

'Abba, Father' (SHF 1)

'Living under the shadow' (SHF 331)

Lively

'Everyone in the whole wide world' (*Jump Up if you're Wearing Red*, p. 2)

'I will enter his gates' (SHF 252)

'He came down' (*Jump Up if you're Wearing Red*, p. 36)

3.   SHARING WITH OTHERS

Intercessions   *Use this beautiful prayer of St Teresa of Avila as a basis for praying for others. You might also wish to use a sung response from Taizé between each short prayer.*

Christ has no body now on earth but yours, no hands but yours, no feet but yours; yours are the eyes through which to look at Christ's compassion to the world, yours are the feet with which he is to go about doing good, and yours are the hands with which he is to bless us now.

Chocolate feast   *Bring back the cooking group to show what they have made. Tell the congregation that they are welcome to share in a chocolate feast at the end of the service.*

Song   'Restore, O Lord' (SHF 464)

CONCLUSION

Final summing up   *Go through the three main points again, reminding everyone of ways we can help each other, the importance of sharing together in worship, and how we can share with others.*

The blessing

Recessional song   *Sing the African song* 'Siyahamba/ We are marching in the light of God' (*Jump Up if you're Wearing Red*, p. 34) *as you leave the church building.*

Chocolate slab recipe

The amounts given may well need doubling, depending on the size of your congregation.

100g (4 oz) margarine or butter
3 tablespoons golden syrup
2 dessertspoons cocoa
75g (3 oz) dried fruit
200g (8 oz) digestive biscuits, crushed
150g (6 oz) chocolate (optional)

Melt the margarine or butter and syrup together. This can either be done in a saucepan on a stove, or, if that is not possible, in a basin over a bowl of hot water, although this will obviously take longer.

Remove from heat and stir in the rest of the ingredients. Press into a baking tray. If you have time, you can melt 150g (6 oz) chocolate and spread it over the top. It should all set fairly quickly. Cut into squares to serve.

Sue and Hamish Bruce

Onesimus

The small book of Philemon is often neglected. Here, the extraordinary story of Onesimus, Philemon's runaway slave, is told.

Bible reference

Philemon

'Come on, get a move on. I can't think why your name is Onesimus.' The master was angry because the slave's name, Onesimus, meant 'useful', but this slave was not a good one. He really was not very useful at all. In fact, after a while he got into trouble.

We don't know quite what Onesimus did. Did he lose some money, or did he steal it?

We know he should have gone straight away and said sorry, even if he was beaten for it. However, he was like you and me. Instead of owning up, we often make matters worse by telling a lie, or even running away. That's just what Onesimus did. He ran away.

He ran away to Rome. Rome was a great city. He thought that no one would find him there. All the same, Onesimus must have been frightened, looking over his shoulder in case someone should recognize him and take him back to his master. If a runaway slave was caught he might have his ear or even his head chopped off. Things were worse now than when he was with his master. He couldn't get work. He was hungry and helpless. He too began to wonder why he had been called 'useful'. Maybe it would have been better if he had been called 'useless'.

The good news is that God did not think he was useless. Perhaps Onesimus was sitting by the riverside when someone spoke to him.

'Listen, boy, I don't know if you are in trouble or not, but I know someone who can help you. Come with me. We are going to listen to a man who tells us about God.'

Strangely, the man took Onesimus to a prison. Yes, even while he was in prison, the apostle Paul was telling people about Jesus Christ. Onesimus stood there with the others and heard how much God loved him, that he would forgive him for all the bad things he had done, and give him new life, because Jesus had died in his place. He learned that though he might be considered useless to men, he was special to God.

Perhaps he stayed behind after the others had gone home, and the prisoner, Paul, helped him, because we know that he prayed, asking the Lord Jesus to forgive him for all the bad things he had done, and to be his Saviour.

After that, Onesimus was so glad to be a Christian that he stayed to look after Paul. Yes, there in prison. We don't know if the guards let him sleep there, but he certainly went there every day. He was very happy to be with Paul, and he tried to forget about his master, and the money.

He tried hard to forget, but he couldn't. He knew that he belonged to his master and that he ought to go back and say sorry. It was a frightening thought. How could he pay back the money he had taken? Perhaps his master would kill him. Besides, who would look after Paul, there in the prison?

I'm sure that Onesimus must have prayed, 'O Lord, please help me to do what you want me to do,' because one day he saw Paul writing a letter. When he had finished, he folded, or maybe rolled it up and gave it to Onesimus.

'Onesimus, this is a letter to your master, Philemon,' he told him. 'Will you take it to him for me?' Then he told him some wonderful news. Philemon was not only a Christian too, but also a friend of Paul's.

Philemon looked hard at him when Onesimus brought him Paul's letter. 'Do you know what Paul has written to me?' he asked. 'He says that you are just like his own son. He says that you aren't useless, but very useful to him, and that you will be to me too. He has asked me to forgive you for what you did. He asks me to treat you like a brother.'

We don't know the end of the story, because the letter that Paul wrote to Onesimus' master is all that we have in the Bible. Perhaps Philemon did send the boy back to Rome to look after Paul. We don't know. But we do know that Onesimus did what God wanted when he went back and said sorry to his master.

I expect people started enjoying calling him Onesimus. He had learned from God and from Paul how to be really useful. Onesimus had a name he could now be proud of.

Pauline Lewis

Revelation

Pictures of heaven

The book of Revelation presents a difficult challenge for the worship leader. How can we use such a complex book in all-age worship? This service provides a simple introduction for both children and all ages to the amazing visual imagery of Revelation.

Bible reference

Revelation

Preparation

- Invite people of all ages to prepare pictures, poems or prose which express their perceptions of heaven. Some might be transferred to acetates where an OHP is available.

- Invite people to present what John saw through the open door (*listed below*) through, for example, choral speaking, sound, pictures, mime, dance.

Welcome and introductory sentence   'After this I looked, and there in heaven a door stood open' (Revelation 4.1a).

Hymn   'Do not be afraid' (HON 111)

Talk   Today's service is based upon a book in the Bible which is full of pictures – 'word pictures' of heaven. The man who wrote it believed that he had seen through an open door into heaven, and he tried to write down what he had seen.

Show some pictures of 'heaven' – any pictures available from libraries of 'the heavens' / space / heaven, as well as pictures prepared by people during previous weeks. Poems or prose could be read aloud too.

If you have an OHP, perhaps some of the pictures could be projected, with appropriate music being played at the same time.

John of Patmos was a prisoner on an island, exiled to that island because he believed in Jesus. He lived in a very cruel time when people could be killed for as little as refusing to bow down to the emperor. His life was so hard that he dreamed of the world as we know it coming to an end and a whole new existence beginning for those who believe in Jesus.

Hymn   'Holy, Holy, Holy' (HON 210)

Talk   Through that open door, this is some of what John of Patmos saw:

These could be called out from different parts of the church, or presented as suggested above.

God coming in on a cloud

People in long robes

'Dazzling faces'

Stars

Swords

Rainbows

Emeralds

Golden crowns

Thrones with thunder and lightning coming from them

Flaming torches

Animals with eyes in the back of their heads

Six-winged beasts

A lamb with seven eyes and seven horns

Harps

People singing and lying flat on their faces before God

Where there is a fairly comfortable feeling about conversation between worship leader and congregation, the following section could be given more time. Otherwise the worship leader could ask these questions rhetorically.

What a picture!

Is it like any of our pictures?

Maybe – maybe not!

Is that where you would like to spend for ever?

Maybe – maybe not!

Well, that is OK. John of Patmos had his picture of heaven and we each have our pictures of heaven.

What is important is to remember that heaven is where God wants us. And God honours our dreams and pictures, delighting in each one of us having the faith to believe in heaven. Our pictures of heaven are as important to God as they are to us.

Hymn 'Be still and know that I am God' (HON 52)

Prayers If you were going somewhere for ever, what would make it 'heavenly'?

In the silence think of:

* Who you would like to have with you
* Which places it would be like
* What things you would do
* How people would behave towards each other.

We thank God for creating us with the capacity to paint pictures in our minds.

We thank God for the people, places and things of this life which are gifts to us for ever.

We thank God that everything we love now and makes us happy now is only a part of all that is promised to us.

The peace

Hymn 'Great is thy faithfulness' (HON 186)

Talk Jesus once said, 'My kingdom is not from this world.' Being with Jesus is very different from what we might expect, so it is very important to enjoy all the pictures of heaven that different people have, whether it is John of Patmos or *N* (*name of someone in the congregation*) because then we will know how to enjoy the surprises that God has in store for us all.

The blessing   'Make way, make way for Christ the King' (HON 329)

Judith Sadler

List of Resources

BBC Come and Praise, BBC Books, 1978.

Derek Haylock, *Plays for all Seasons,* National Society/Church House Publishing, 1997.

Dave Hopwood, *Playing Up*, National Society/Church House Publishing, 1998.

Hymns Ancient and Modern New Standard, Hymns Ancient and Modern Limited, 1983.

Hymns for Today's Church, Hodder & Stoughton, 1982.

Hymns Old and New, New Anglican Edition, Kevin Mayhew, 1996.

Jump Up if you're Wearing Red, National Society/Church House Publishing, 1996.

Junior Praise, Combined Music Edition, Marshall Pickering, 1997.

Mission Praise, Marshall Pickering, 1986.

Michael Perry (ed.), *Church Family Worship,* Hodder & Stoughton, 1986.

Michael Perry (ed.), *The Dramatised Bible*, Marshall Pickering and Bible Society, 1989.

Songs and Hymns of Fellowship, Integrated Music Edition, Kingsway Music, 1987.

Susan Sayers, *Living Stones: Complete Resource Book*, Kevin Mayhew, 1997.

Ruth Tiller, *Keeping the Feast: Seasonal Dramas for All-age Worship*, Kevin Mayhew, 1995.

Worship through the Christian Year: Year C, National Society/Church House Publishing, 1997.

Together with Children

*I*f you have found the material in this book useful, why not subscribe to the parent magazine?

Together with Children provides practical, topical resource material, information about wider issues in Christian children's work, and inspiration for leaders. Every issue contains:

- A COMPLETE ALL-AGE SERVICE

- ONE OR MORE STORIES

- SKETCHES FOR CHILDREN TO PERFORM OR WATCH

- AN ARTICLE ABOUT AN ISSUE IN CHILDREN'S WORK

- A REPORT OF GOOD WORK BEING DONE

- BOOK REVIEWS

There are also activity ideas for a saint's day or festival, readers' letters and an opinion column.

FREE sample copies are available from the National Society at the address below.

ANNUAL SUBSCRIPTIONS (9 issues per year: monthly during school term), are available from The National Society, Church House, Great Smith Street, London SW1P 3NZ.

DISCOUNTS are available for multiple-copy subscriptions going to the same address (e.g. for two leaders working together, or for one of the clergy as well as the children's leader). For more details contact: The National Society, Church House, Great Smith Street, London, SW1P 3NZ. Telephone: 0171 222 1672; Fax: 0171 233 2592; e-mail: info@natsoc.org.zuk.

Together for Festivals

Edited by
Pam Macnaughton

The *Together for Festivals* anthology groups together some of the best resource ideas from the last three years of the magazine *Together with Children* with previously unpublished material.

It includes drama sketches, all-age services, stories, craft ideas and group activities placed in the following sections:

- ADVENT AND CHRISTMAS
- EPIPHANY
- CANDALMAS
- PENTECOST
- LENT AND EASTER
- ALL SAINTS

Together for Festivals offers highly practical suggestions for leaders to help all young (of every age!) to celebrate the main festivals of the Christian Year. Illustrated throughout by Simon Smith, this is a 'must have' for children's leaders, clergy and all those involved in all-age worship.

ISBN 0 7151 4893 1

£9.95